# Selma's
# SELF-SACRIFICE

Rev. Dr. Frederick D. Reese

Kathy M. Walters

Library of Congress Cataloging-in-Publication Data
Reese, Rev. Dr. Frederick D.
Selma's Self-Sacrifice Rev. Dr. Frederick D. Reese and
Kathy M. Walters

1. Reese, Frederick D. 2. Black History 3. Selma, Alabama
4. Teachers March 5. Walters, Kathy M.

ISBN 978-0-578-46044-4

# DEDICATION

I dedicate this book to:
Alline, my wonderful wife of 64 years,
my family and the people of Selma.

# SPECIAL NOTE

This book references and contains the words: "black," "black people," "blacks," "white," "white people," "whites," and the words "nigger" and "niggers" to describe individuals as they were referenced specifically during this time period. Neither the terms nor the intent is meant to degrade or offend the reader. These references depict the descriptive labels used in Selma and beyond. Then, and unfortunately, now.

# CONTENTS

How can we thrive when the story is untold?
How do we go forth without history to behold?
Why can't we be strong and rise from defeat?
Why don't we build a bridge of love... made of liberty,
justice, equality and peace?

Kathy M. Walters

# FOREWORD

By Althelstein Johnson

From obscurity to notoriety to celebrity represents the life cycle of Frederick Douglas Reese, civil rights activist and icon. Born in Selma, AL, a relatively unknown small town in the Black Belt, Fred was primarily a number in the census. His parentage was humble, a typical Negro boy born into a family of two older sisters and a mother closely connected to an extended family support group. Despite the ordinary, his humble beginning was somewhat unordinary, and his accomplishments were extraordinary. Fred's immediate family valued and stressed the importance of education. His mother was a teacher. She, along with other family members, planted seeds of awareness and encouragement, which germinated in Fred during his early years. Fred attended school regularly and mastered the basics without intense study. He was considered an "apt" student, one blessed with alertness and quick comprehension and retention. Without much ado and within normalcy, Fred navigated through his primary grades largely unnoticed.

Upon reaching adolescence, Fred exerted his manly attributes. A legend within his own era and among his peers, he "lived up to" and justified his reputation of "not backing down" and "holding his own." Physical prowess outweighed moral and Christian allegiance instilled from birth. Fred engaged in some juvenile entanglements, which proved him to "live up to" his reputation. Divine intervention, or prayers answered, or maturation and growth, all may have contributed to the change in Fred. Not a man of physical might, but a gentleman of moral valor and principle, Fred began to practice his principles. The dramatic and perhaps traumatic occurrence of his transition came unannounced and unanticipated. It happened on the "Downing Ground," a small, central area of the playground, respected by all of the students as almost hallowed ground on the campus of Knox Academy, the junior high he attended. Fred's epiphany occurred as a shower of rain on a humid midday. He was challenged to prove himself as either the victor or victim of a dispute. During his potential violent response, he was overcome by a voice that said to him: "Put your arms down and walk away, not cowardly but courageously, and nonviolently." From this moment to the end of his life, Fred carried the mantle of nonviolence bravely and boldly.

Gradually and genuinely, Fred's transformation was taking place. It began to manifest itself in his actions and interactions. His college years at Alabama State University record him as a standout student recognized for his scholarship, commensurate to an athlete's athleticism. Fred's professors nurtured his aptitude and affinity for moral integrity, human equality and social responsibility. His engagement with human advocates and historical leaders through readings and his involvement in campus civic and social events catapulted the formation of his pervasive personal and political agenda.

Following his return to his hometown, Fred began his educational career at Millers Ferry as a teacher. Former students remember him as a strict disciplinarian, knowledgeable instructor and compassionate human being. His career kick-off was also the site where he met and married the love of his life, Alline Crossing. The union produced five children and 64 years of bliss, lasting to his demise.

Selma, the place of his birth and obscurity, became the site of his notoriety and ultimately his celebrity status. F. D. Reese, "the man in the making," soon became "the man known around the nation" for his response to the segregated practices of his city. He, along with others – especially the Courageous Eight and coworkers in the Selma Teachers Association – actively protested the Jim Crow system passionately, persistently and nonviolently, advocating for justice and equality.

A highlight of Dr. Reese's life occurred when he and other marchers were confronted on the Edmund Pettus Bridge by Selma patrolmen and Alabama state troopers in a melee now infamously known as Bloody Sunday. Later, Dr. Reese recalled the irony of the situation: "As a schoolboy, I went to the dedication of the Edmund Pettus Bridge fascinated by the fanfare of it all; now, on this same bridge I was brutally attacked as a citizen exercising rights I learned as a student."

*Selma's Self-Sacrifice* is a compelling narrative of the life of Rev. Dr. Frederick Douglas Reese, known by many epithets, but most appropriately and humbly as *servant leader*. In his own words, unadulterated and without embellishment, he shares his story, a testament and record of a life well-lived.

Kathy M. Walters has become the voice of an unsung hero of the civil rights era from a local, national and global perspective. In a conversational tone, she allows the reader to listen to the authentic voice of Dr. Reese, just as he spoke directly to many who came from far and near to hear him tell his story – which now becomes an integral part of our history as a nation.

# THE TEACHERS
# MARCH

"*The* Lord had me at the right place, at the right time, for the right commitment."

Rev. Dr. Frederick D. Reese

"*Get off these steps right now! Get away! You heard me! Why are you here?*"

"*We're here so we can go into our courthouse and file applications so we can become registered voters.*"

"*Go! Gather up your teachers and take 'em back to the school where they came from! You hear me?*"

"*This courthouse does not belong to you, Sheriff Clark. This courthouse belongs to all of us. And as citizens of this county, we're here to see if the Board of Registrars is in session. We have a right to enter into this courthouse, and we will not back down from that right.*"

"*Well, the registrar's office is not open on Fridays for voter registration,*" Sheriff Clark scoffed. "*And you're making a mockery out of my courthouse.*"

Immediately, we could feel the heat of an unwelcoming atmosphere. Absorbed in a tense and tumultuous storm, we witnessed bolts of lightning and heard the reverberating rumbles

1

emanating from the Sheriff and his posse as they showered us with the brew of their uttered disdain. Though the weather that day was relatively cool and calm, we knew we were in the middle of a sweltering storm, and we were certain its intensity wouldn't subside any time soon.

Sheriff Jim Clark was infamous for his radical views and vicious actions against racial integration. Exhibiting his militant approach and extreme forces and tactics against blacks, he never hesitated to use his billy club to execute control. Sheriff Clark perceived blacks as sub-standard and non-factors of society. Many who were remotely familiar with Selma, Alabama equated Sheriff Clark to a brandishing force to be reckoned with. He was eager to inflict pain, and he was never reticent of his standing as a proponent of segregation. Garnishing his military-type uniform was a button that he wore with both pride and conviction. It read: "NEVER," referencing his disapproval for granting civil or political rights to blacks. Nearly every black person in or near Selma was familiar with, had witnessed first-hand or had heard mention of Sheriff Jim Clark.

So, as President of the Selma City Teachers Association, I had challenged all teachers to participate in the right to vote campaign. In the months preceding the event, I had led numerous meetings to educate, empower and ignite some of the flames from a fire burning deep inside me, so that the importance of participating in the voting process would spread like a brushfire. My goal was to let teachers know that one of our most prized possessions is our voice, and to stress the potential impact we could have by taking a stand and fighting for what was rightfully ours.

Each meeting began and ended with prayer. My prayers were yielded to strengthen our faith and ask for God's guidance as we embarked upon the task. This platform also provided informational and question-and-answer sessions and served an outlet to discuss not only the disconcerting climate in Selma, but also our future plans of action. I stressed the importance of the right to vote, and I knew that as a group, we had to push past the obstacles that we would inevitably encounter. Not only would we fight for those rights, but we would be educated about the purpose for doing so. The population in Selma was majority black, but one could not decipher that by viewing the political rosters. And the absence of blacks in the political process would mean the absence of progress in our civil rights efforts.

The act of discrimination against blacks was rampant and in the forefront throughout many periods of history. It is specifically earmarked from 1877 through the 1960s under the existence of the Jim Crow Laws. Jim Crow Laws loomed heavily over the South during this time frame. These laws enforced racial segregation due to whites' perception that blacks were dirty, unworthy, insignificant or simply viewed as "not good enough" to integrate with the white population. Whites did not want to go to school or church with us. We could not drink from the same water fountains, swim in the same pools, eat at the same restaurants or use the same public restroom facilities. And these exclusions are merely to name a few. During those times in the past, it was neither uncommon nor unheard of to see the following verbiage proudly posted outside of many establishments owned by whites:

# "WHITES ONLY"

# "NO COLOREDS ALLOWED"

# "WE ONLY SERVE WHITES"

# "NO BLACKS"

The climate was quite dark for black people in Selma and neighboring locales in the south. Layered with the harsh treatment evoked and executed as a result of the Jim Crow Laws, Selma was also exercising under an injunction imposed by Circuit Court Judge James Hare. The injunction prohibited mass meetings in churches and banned groups of three or more individuals associated with civil rights groups from congregating at mass meetings or on the streets of Selma. This injunction was first placed into force in the second quarter of 1964.

Many black teachers and the black citizens of Selma were afraid to attend the planned and sometimes impromptu meetings for our discussion platforms. The fear of losing homes and jobs and suffering public ridicule by whites was a consequence many blacks did not wish to face. This was a valid fear, because once word got out that "this black person" or "that black person" had been seen attending meetings or attempting to register to vote, that's exactly what might have happened. But then there were those of us who were willing to fight fearlessly, in spite of our fears.

In a meeting held in the cafeteria of R.B. Hudson High School, I persuaded the teachers of Selma to sign a petition to march for voters' rights. My execution of the Teachers March was not to be viewed as just another march. I wasn't attempting to engage the teachers in an activity without merit or reason. My thought process was generated with purpose and conviction. And I definitely had what the young people call "receipts" to substantiate the success of my prior demands for justice, and I was fighting for justice with the ultimate goal of having those demands granted.

The teachers of Selma were well aware of my unwavering fights on their behalf. In prior years, black female teachers were not granted the benefits of maternity leave or sick leave. White female teachers, on the other hand, could automatically look forward to those benefits the moment they discovered they were with child. White female teachers had the privilege of giving birth to their precious babies and were allowed to recuperate for several weeks while their bodies healed before returning to their teaching jobs. They were also allowed to utilize time off whenever they were ill. However, black female teachers were virtually ignored and intentionally unrecognized when they needed time off for childbirth. God help them if they got up one morning and felt sick. Black female teachers were forced to take time off without pay, either returning to work well before their bodies had properly healed or forced to vacate their jobs altogether. Frankly, they were often fired. This unequal treatment was unjustified. All women – white, black, blue, brown, red or rainbow – should be allowed the time needed for nurturing, and for the overall care and bonding time with their newborn babies. Black female teachers voiced their desire to be granted just a few

5

weeks' leave for nature's healing, as well as necessary adjustments to the new world of motherhood. Some women experienced complications and some unfortunately experienced the loss of a baby during or shortly after birth and needed time to grieve their loss. I knew that I couldn't settle in the seat of complacency. I had to do something to help fight for the teachers.

I voiced my opinion to the Superintendent, the School Board and anyone else within earshot. I fought and I kept fighting, unafraid to stand up for yet another disparaging imbalance of justice. Days, weeks and months passed, wherein I spoke with the black female teachers and assured them that I was in their corner. I continued to raise the topic at every school meeting and every board meeting, bringing awareness and generating a voice that the black female teachers were afraid to exercise on their own behalf. Whenever we convened, I would stand up to speak. I used my leverage as President of the Teachers Association, and I took my position seriously. After some time had passed, the board members were well aware of the main item I was there to discuss. I can recall the time when I stood up to speak and a board member sighed and looked up at the ceiling as he spoke, "Reese, do you have anything new to address today?" I completely ignored his comment and proceeded to discuss maternity leave. At other meetings, I was informed that the maternity leave issue was not on the agenda, or that we didn't have time to add it to the agenda, or I was simply asked to sit down. There was no way that I would sit down when I knew I had to stand up for what was right. After one meeting in particular, I thought to myself, "They have no idea who they are dealing with. If they are under the assumption that I will give up, they are in for a rude awakening." I was shamelessly relentless. They continued to add fuel to the fire. I kept standing. Meeting after meeting, I would stand. And once all was said and done, I imagine the "powers that be" knew that I wouldn't shut up, so they gave up. The final time I stood up to speak, the board agreed to extend maternity leave to the black female teachers! One could not tell from the outside, but inside I was ecstatic. I felt so proud relaying the news to the teachers. "I have some exciting news to share to all of you," I told them. "Maternity leave and sick leave are now being extended to you all." Hands down. The battle was won.

So, when I presented my concept of a Teachers March and the word began to spread, many of the teachers supported me because they knew of my track record. You didn't need to hand me the baton. Once I saw it, I would take it and run with it! Most knew that I had fire inside of me. They knew that I had a zeal for fighting for justice, and they also knew that I would utilize every muscle in my body to fight for justice. Not for one, but for all. I wanted teachers to join me and fight as a group. Collectively, we would make a statement and fight for what was rightfully ours. And that was the right to vote! During the time of the Teachers March, I was already a registered voter. But teachers as a whole were not registered. Some teachers had been turned down numerous times after appearing in the registrar's office and were denied the right to vote over and over again. I was determined to get these teachers in one accord and standing together. And until all teachers were registered voters and granted the right to participate in the political process, I could not sit still.

*"We as teachers should teach by precepts and examples."* My goal was to be as forthcoming as possible. Words without action were tantamount to accepting our denial of rights. I then posed the charging question: *"How can we convincingly teach good citizenship when we are not first-class citizens ourselves?"* At that moment, the teachers embraced the challenge. Many expressed their approval with applause, and others rose to their feet and yelled with enthusiasm. I saw smiles on a lot of faces. After the cheers, chants and declaration of our upcoming victory, I asked the teachers to settle down a bit. "Okay, teachers. We're starting to behave like some of our students." They laughed. "It's time to get to work!"

And so it was. *"The teachers of Selma will engage in a Teachers March to the Voter registrar's office located in the Dallas County Courthouse on January 22, 1965,"* I announced. And for the first time in U.S. history, teachers would engage in a march for the right to vote!

On January 22, 1965, the morning of the march, I awoke with renewed strength. I had had a restful sleep the night before, and I knew that God would be marching with me as I led the teachers on our journey. You see, I always maintained a close relationship with the Lord. I talked to him before I went to bed at night, and I covered myself with the armor of God when I arose and throughout every waking hour. My prayers, devotional bible readings and simple thanks to him for another day, always drew me closer to God.

Dear Eternal God, my Heavenly Father, I come to
you this day to give you all the thanks, all the glory

8

and all the honor. I thank you for waking me up this morning. I thank you for renewed strength. I thank you for giving me the will to fight for what is right and stand for what I truly believe in. I ask that you walk with us on this journey to the courthouse today. I ask that you cover and keep us. Let your will be done. In the mighty name of Jesus, Amen!

I knew that I had prepared myself and the teachers for this day, and I was ready to face the fire. As I stood up to proceed to the front of the house for breakfast, I hummed and softly sang one of my favorite hymns, *I Need Thee Every Hour:*

I need Thee, Oh

I need Thee

Every hour, I need Thee

Oh, bless me now, my Savior!

I come to Thee

Gracefully and delicately moving around in the kitchen was my beautiful wife, Alline. She looked over at me when I walked into the kitchen, and her lips curled into one of her famously beautiful smiles. I nearly staggered as I inhaled the aroma from my favorite hot breakfast: flapjacks, eggs over easy, grits and sausage. Alline always prepared phenomenal meals, but it seemed as though she added an extra flare and an extra touch of love whenever I was preparing to go out for a meeting, or when she knew that I would be facing the opposition. I gave her a kiss and sat down at the table. She prepared my plate, then hers, and we enjoyed a lovely breakfast.

"It's time for me to head out, Alline."

"Okay, Frederick. Be safe."

I left my home thanking God for a supportive wife and a satisfying meal! I also prayed that He would cover me and my home while I was away.

⁓

I completed my teaching duties at R.B. Hudson High School around 3 p.m. and proceeded to Clark Elementary School to meet with the teachers. Lawrence Huggins, Sally Surrency Jackson, Elmyra Martin Smith and Sarah Carter Craig were some of the teachers marching that day. Margaret Moore helped organize. We assembled on the upper level of the school. This place was nostalgic for me because I'd attended classes at Clark Elementary from grades one through six. I always recognized that change was necessary, and deep down, I knew it was up to me to make a difference. My humble beginnings were now coming full circle as I was about to lead the teachers of Selma to what I knew I was destined to concert. I was happy to see a few of my former teachers at the meeting. One of my grade school teachers advised me that he was there to offer his support, but he was unable to march. He was a bit up in age, and his physical abilities weren't as agile as they once were. I expressed my gratitude for the mere thought of him being there. And he assured me that he would remain in that same spot until he witnessed myself and the teachers' safe return to Clark Elementary School.

We knew in advance that everyone was not supporting the march and there was an array of opinions. Some residents of Selma expressed their thoughts early on, stating that they didn't believe the march would ever leave the ground. Others were fearful that if they participated in the march, they would be at risk of losing their homes and jobs and would be subjected to ridicule or outcast. Some had no opinion at all and preferred to just wait and see what transpired. Nevertheless, we also heard from those who were hopeful and supportive and couldn't wait until the march began.

Prior to walking out of the school, I read a scripture and asked for God's grace as I led the marchers in prayer:

Dear Eternal God, our Heavenly Father, we come to you this day to give you all the thanks, all the glory, all the honor and, most of all, Lord, all the praise. We thank you for bringing us here today. We thank you for waking us up this morning in our right minds and with a purpose in our hearts. We thank you for strength. We thank you for the parameters of peace. We thank you for giving us the will to fight for what is right and stand for what we believe in. We ask that you walk with us on this journey today. Cover us and keep us. Let your will be done. In the Mighty name of Jesus, we pray. AMEN!

I had a peaceful night's sleep prior to the morning of the Teachers March. I awoke with renewed strength, and I knew that God would be marching with me as I led the teachers to the steps of the courthouse. You see, I always maintained a close relationship with the Lord. I talked to Him before I went to bed each night, and I always asked Him to cover me throughout my day. I didn't know what the outcome of the march would be, but I had faith in the one who held the outcome in the palm of His hands.

The school doors began to continuously sway back and forth as teachers, members of the community and supporters arrived. Each person who entered the school would shake hands with other supporters, peer around the room and wave, or embrace and smile at the many familiar faces. The crowd grew, and the energy level was positively high. Slowly, one by one, everyone took a seat and finally settled in. Upon doing so, the room's energy shifted. As I panned around the room, I noticed that many marchers appeared to be frozen in deep thought, perhaps pensive about what we might face once we left the school. I observed some individuals with their eyes closed as they silently prayed, while others stood with their arms outstretched, as they prayed openly. I looked over at Mr. A.J. Durgan and nodded my head. He recognized the gesture as a cue that I was ready to begin. I cleared my throat as I approached the podium.

"May I have everyone's attention, please? Let us bow our heads for a word of prayer."

I prayed for the march, I prayed for the marchers and I also prayed for victory. I thanked everyone for coming out to demonstrate their support by participating in the march. After sharing words of encouragement and conducting a brief question and answer session, I cleared my throat again as I concluded with the final instructions. My faith was strong, and I took comfort in knowing that God would be with us every step of the way. I closed my eyes and had another quick and personal talk with God before leading the marches out of the doors of the church. I felt calm, and I was pleased with how everything had fallen into place thus far. And I knew deep down inside that everything would be alright.

Two by two, we marched out of the schoolyard from Lawrence Street to Alabama Avenue and proceeded to the courthouse. I had instructed everyone to walk out with their heads high as we exited the school. And as for me, fear was nowhere to be found. As we placed one foot in front of the other, focused on a venture never taken, we were amazed at the response we received shortly after the march began.

As we marched, our footsteps could be heard like an army of soldiers marching to battle. We witnessed numbers of people running out of their houses and onto the sidewalk to cheer us on. Some people waved and jumped for joy, yelling from the top of their lungs. Some smiled as they waved, and we graciously smiled and waved back. I saw grandmothers sitting on their porches, and I saw parents cradling their children while they cheered us on. I even saw some who were weeping and thanking God as we traveled past them. What touched me the most were the people I recognized that had been arrested during the past year or so and had experienced hardship due to being arrested numerous times. They'd fought, marched and protested, and some of those were the ones who had lost jobs or suffered backlash as a result. Teachers, on the other hand, and the more "educated" blacks in Selma hadn't experienced backlash to the degree they had. Teachers had never marched before, never protested and never placed their stance in the forefront. And for those individuals to hear that the teachers would be marching and to witness the great number of us marching for them, they were crying tears of joy. And it's rumored that one of the teachers spotted an older couple dancing with their canes, holding onto the fence as they danced the "Jitterbug!"

We were humbled by the display of approval being demonstrated by so many as we moved throughout the neighborhood surrounding Brown Chapel Church. But our exuberance was short-lived. Soon after we reached the areas more populated by whites, and passed by the business district, our reception was juxtaposed by sneers, name calling and stares by the white residents and white business owners.

"You colored folks are a disgrace! Stop wastin' your time!"

"You niggers need to go home!"

"Go home, niggers!"

"Hey, nigger teachers! Why can't y'all learn how to leave well enough alone? Go teach that! Nasty niggers."

It's a stretch to say this, but the comments I've referenced are the most family-friendly remarks that I can repeat from what I heard that day. And with none of the statements reflecting either "family" or "friendly" references, I can only shake my head as I relive that moment. And I won't dignify the more repulsive, odious remarks by repeating them in this book. I was shocked to see the number of white people who were dropping what they were doing to display their disapproval. They were walking out of their homes and businesses, yelling as loud as they could. This was a stark contrast to the positive responses we had received after leaving the school. This response differed because we were now being taunted. Whites were walking alongside us as we marched, but their intent was strictly to intimidate. In addition to being called vulgar names, I saw whites waving sticks and any other object they could grab as a threat to evoke fear and to coerce us into going away. One older gentleman was so furious, you could see food particles exploding from his mouth as he spat words of hate. Apparently, he felt compelled to abandon his meal at the restaurant, rise from the table and step outside to call us every name but a child of God. Some whites were yelling negative comments. We were met with such severe expletives and disrespectful comments that some of the teachers paused dead in their tracks as a result of shock and disbelief. Many teachers were not accustomed to this harsh, never-before experienced confrontation. The whites who weren't verbalizing or waving sticks as a show of their disapproval of our march were displaying obscene hand gestures, followed by narrow-eyed, threatening stares. The teachers had been holding up well since the beginning of the march, but there are thresholds to the limits of what any one person can take. I felt that this harsh treatment was beginning to take a toll on my fellow teachers. I was sensitive to their feelings, and I knew I had to check in for a quick pep talk and let them know that we could get through this. Mostly, I wanted to let them know that I cared.

I looked over at Mr. Durgan and I nodded. He nodded back

and swept his open hand in a slow, outward motion, and said, "Go ahead." He wasn't walking as fast as he was before. And immediately after he made his statement, his feet rested to a complete stop. So did mine. I knew him so well and we had such a connection that I think we could read each other's minds. Mr. Durgan stood alongside my right shoulder and flashed a very slight smile to the teachers, waiting for me to speak. I smiled slightly as I faced the teachers, making eye contact with all in view. "I know we're facing a tough crowd today," I told them. "This is a first for us as a group, and right now, it's not looking very pretty. They are really trying our patience. It is going to get tougher before it gets better. But let's keep marching. I know it's been rough for many of you, but we're almost at the courthouse. I've faced this type of treatment, so I'm accustomed to it. You're not, and I understand. We will press on. We will stand for what's right. We will not let them stop us. God is in control."

I heard some chattering among some of the teachers after I spoke. I knew this wasn't easy. I could see tears in the eyes of a few of the teachers, while the words of encouragement seemed to give others a burst of will and determination. My goal was to help eliminate the fear and offer a sense of confidence. We brushed off the dust, and we kept marching. I knew the last several minutes were emotionally challenging for the teachers. But I also knew that as the leader, I had to keep the faith and maintain control. I was walking and praying the entire time: *God, please make us strong. Give us the strength we need to fight this fight. Make us unmovable, undeterred and unstoppable. In Jesus' name, I pray. Amen.*

When we reached our destination, we could see that all of

the major news outlets were at the courthouse. Broadcasting and bracing for stories were NBC, CBS and ABC. We had no idea that the Teachers March would be getting worldwide coverage. I never envisioned that the march I organized with the teachers of Selma would be captured by the eyes of the nation. Their eyes were on Selma. Their eyes were on the teachers. Now, their eyes were on me. Atop the courthouse steps stood the infamous Sheriff Jim Clark and his posse. Sheriff Clark and his posse were always front and center when it came to taunting blacks. Awaiting our arrival at the bottom of the steps were the Superintendent of Education and the Chairman of the Board of Education. I had interacted with both men on occasion, prior to the march. They were not strangers to me. Our interactions, though minimal, were seemingly cordial. They respected me, and I respected them as well. But this mission was not about respect. It was about justice. These two men were there to persuade me to discontinue the march and force myself, Mr. Durgan and the teachers to turn on our heels and head back to Clark Elementary School. Their goal was to stop us dead in our tracks. By no means would I allow them to subjugate our cause. We wouldn't give up that easily. The Chairman of the Board said to me, "You've made your point, Mr. Reese. You've made your point. So please, take these teachers back to the school. There's no need to pursue."

Focused and determined to do what the teachers and I set out to accomplish, I responded to the man who signed my check, "We have a right to be here. This is our courthouse. Please step aside."

*"You got exactly one minute to move before me and my deputies make you move!"* the sheriff spat.

17

Not one sound. No one moved. I knew we had a mission to fulfill. Regardless of the sheriff's gruff tone and condescending retort toward myself, the teachers and additional participants in this march, we would not back down. Every citizen has a right to vote. Teachers who held Bachelor's and Master's degrees were encouraged and challenged to file applications at the Dallas County Courthouse to become registered voters. But that was a feat with seemingly insurmountable odds. Twice, I had appeared before the Board of Registrars in order to be allowed to take the written and oral tests required for voter registration. And after I became a registered voter, I encouraged every teacher to do the same. I couldn't fathom how Selma's school system could be inundated with highly skilled and educated teachers, and yet they remain disenfranchised. *How could we allow that to be? How can this continue?* Denying our right to register to vote was an injustice that we would no longer tolerate. *We must continue the fight for our right to vote*, I thought to myself.

At the expiration of one minute, Sheriff Clark and his deputies, who had now moved from blocking the doorways, lunged forward and jabbed us down the steps and onto the sidewalk. Mr. A.J. Durgan, my double-file marching partner, former Science teacher from grades ten through twelve and the one helping lead the march, was not accustomed to this type of treatment. He glanced at me with slightly raised brows, and from the corner of his large, inquisitive eyes he asked silently, "What shall we do?"

With limited expression, I simply glanced back at him, "We are going back."

Closed-mouthed, perplexed and, as if to verify that he heard me correctly, he replied, "Hnnnh?" Mr. Durgan's stance was not that of tepidness or trepidation. He was merely asking so that he could align himself with my next move.

To demonstrate our strong will and undying purpose, we marched back up the steps for the second time. Mr. Durgan maintained his position alongside me. Immediately, we were accosted with more jabbing blows by the billy clubs, forcing us back onto the sidewalk by our oppressors.

Reminiscent of déjà vu or watching an instant replay, Mr. Durgan looked at me and again posed the question, "What shall we do?"

I gave him the same response as before, and he gave me the same reply as before.

"We are going back."

"Hnnnh?

Between 1962 and 1963, Dallas County, Alabama had less than 300 registered black voters who were 18 years of age or older. These were dismal statistics, because the potential black voting age population was 15,000. Prior to this march, I communicated to young citizens 18 and older about the significance of participating in the political process on a local, state and national level. In that quest for obtaining voting rights, scores of young people were arrested and detained in the city/county jails, and the overflow of arrested demonstrators was taken to Camp Selma Prison and placed in degrading holding facilities. But those facts did not sway our motion.

As we regrouped and ascended the steps of the courthouse for the third time, Jim Clark indicated that if we did not get off the steps in one minute, he would arrest us. I thought to myself, *That's exactly what I want you to do. Please. Arrest us.* I had already been in counsel with a lawyer. So I was prepared to be arrested and go to jail that Friday, remain in jail the entire weekend and be released at some point on Sunday. This would allow us time to readjust and be back in our classrooms first thing Monday morning. Most teachers were equipped with a toothbrush and facecloth in preparation for being arrested. I'm certain that the higher ranks in Selma didn't expect teachers to band together in order for our voices to be heard. And I'm also certain they weren't anticipating that we would come out in such great numbers, making such an impactful statement. We clearly demonstrated our intentions. Our jail time would have resulted in a detrimental economic blow, and the system was not prepared for the aftermath.

These scenarios most likely surfaced within the minds of Selma officials, because while we were in a donnybrook with Sheriff Clark, he was suddenly summoned inside the courthouse. Someone from the inside desperately needed to speak with him.

Mr. Durgan, myself and the teachers waited patiently for the outcome of this sudden shift of events. As if time had stopped, so did the dialogue and movement among the marchers as the Sheriff spoke to the unnamed individual. The duration of the conversation was brief. Nevertheless, upon Sheriff Clark's return to the courthouse steps, it was obvious that the threat of our impending arrests no longer existed. The tone shifted. The mood was surprisingly less vile and slightly less commandeering.

"Teachers, you are to end this march and exit the premises.

Leave this courthouse now!" We were jabbed down the steps for the third and final time. This confirmed that we would not be arrested. No additional force. No retaliation from either side. I didn't hear the conversation between Sheriff Clark and the courthouse official who spoke with him inside the courthouse, but I could imagine the official saying, "Sheriff, for goodness sake, don't arrest those teachers."

I was fully aware that the registrar's office would be closed on the day of the march. The registrar's office was always closed on Fridays. In addition, the registrar's office was only open on the first and third Mondays. I had previously written a letter to the Chairman of the Board of Directors requesting consideration that the registrar's office provide greater availability in terms of hours. I believed that if we could go into the courthouse any day of the week for them to take our money for tax payments, we should be allowed the same allotment of time to register to vote.

But my plan that day at the courthouse was specific and strategic. You see, teachers represented the largest black professional organization in the Selma/Dallas County area. We possessed notable measures of buying power, and our arrests would result in a significant loss of revenue for local business establishments. Teachers frequented many restaurants and shops as part of our daily activities, whether school was in session or out of session. And because of the substantial amount of money we spent in Selma, the impact of our arrests would have been tremendous. The absence of "teacher dollars" would have caused an economic collapse in the community. The chain reaction of our arrests would have resulted in thousands of children arriving at their respective Selma district schools without their educators there to teach them. This would have been both chaotic and problematic. And if teachers were arrested, as detainees, they would need to be transported to various holding locations. This means of transport was the practice exercised with past marches due to overflow, and Selma was not prepared to seamlessly manage this set of circumstances. Therefore, the outlined consequences of arresting the teachers would have backfired. So, the decision to refrain from arresting the teachers outweighed the intended punishment for protesting. We weren't granted access to the courthouse that day, but we used our voices and our outward expression of protest. And although we were prepared, we weren't arrested.

As we left the courthouse, we walked away with pride. Although we were not allowed inside the courthouse to address the registrar's office on that day, we knew we were not exiting in vain. One day we would walk back into that office and would secure the approval for everyone, regardless of skin color, who was of legal age of 18 or older to be prideful in the opportunity to exercise their right to vote.

Many citizens walked alongside us from the courthouse to Brown Chapel Church, where it was decided we would convene after the march. That is, unless we were arrested. Many citizens of Selma doubted the Teachers March would ever leave the ground. On so many occasions we faced naysayers and those who doubted the march would be beneficial if we were to execute it. But we didn't blink an eye to those who did not believe in us, our mission or our cause. *"If God is for us, who could be against us?"* (Romans 8:31 NKJV)

And once we arrived at Brown Chapel after marching to and from the courthouse, we were received with a Hero's Welcome by the community and other citizens who had filled the church to capacity.

As we looked around and took in the large crowd, we were ecstatic by the support. There were so many people at the church who now supported us. Our demonstration of unity and purpose transformed the minds of those who previously doubted us. Our former opponents and hecklers in the audience were now supporting actors in our phenomenal reality, simply entitled the Teachers March. And there was standing room only. What an accomplishment. What a feat!

I veered toward the area of the church where my grade school teacher and I last spoke. And there he was. Just as he had promised. We linked eyes, and his expression spoke volumes without saying one single word. I knew he was proud.

I was about to begin the closing prayer when I heard a voice from the front section of the church. One of the mothers began singing one of her favorite songs. The entire church joined in. Whenever someone sings from the bottom of their heart, the spirit moves in a mighty way! The mother rocked and sang, and the entire church joined in! We ended up having a praise session that could be heard by the angels in heaven above. What a mighty God we serve!

On that date, January 22, 1965, after marching through neighborhoods of supporters, being confronted with haters and squaring off nose to nose and face to face with Sheriff Clark, our voices were heard, and our point was definitely made.

The Teachers March was a success! It sparked momentum and boosted participation within many demographics in the fight against political and racial injustice.

This day was one of many that made an indelible mark amidst a sea of memories that will never disappear.

# THE EARLY YEARS

*"How far you go in life depends on your being tender with the young, compassionate with the aged, sympathetic with the striving and tolerant of the weak and strong. Because someday in your life, you will have been all of these."*

George Washington Carver

I entered this world on November 28, 1929, in Selma, Alabama. I was born to a single mother, Ellie R. Reese, and my father, Solomon Cooper, alias George Reese. We lived in a small in-way, also known as a "shotgun" house. A shotgun house is a narrow home where each room is built directly behind another in a straight line. A door is usually stationed at each end of the house. The term shotgun is derived from the thought that if someone fired a shotgun, the bullet would go straight through, traveling from the front door right out the back. Or vice versa. Our two-bedroom home was painted with the hint of a light, smoky gray. There were about three steps leading from the ground to the entryway. The roof was slanted and perfectly etched. The interior was always clean, and the exterior was quaint in adornment. The house was extremely small, given the ratio of family members to

25

available space, but needless to say, this place we called home was filled with so much love.

Our home was located at 916 Minter Avenue, near Tabernacle Baptist Church in Selma, Alabama. Tabernacle was a medium-sized church within the neighborhood. It was notable for community outreach and the undeniable warmth within its membership. My mother made certain that my siblings and I attended church each and every Sunday, and she wouldn't have it any other way. We were taught early on about God and His existence, and how we should always do what was right in His sight. We didn't have much, so we were also taught to place value on the things that really mattered. Our charge was to focus on what was on the inside rather than what we may or may not be wearing on the outside. Growing up, I was a member of Green Street Baptist Church. During service, we were instructed to be quiet when the preacher was preaching. Without question, it was a requirement that we attended Sunday school and church each and every Sunday, and it was mandatory that we always maintained a sense of decorum when in the house of the Lord. I was compliant the majority of the time, but once I grew older, I "accidentally" became a bit unruly. I facetiously describe it as an "accident" because we all know that I knew better! And there were some occasions when my friends and I would pretend to go into the church, but instead go around back and have loads of fun playing outside. Boys will be boys. So, what can I say?

We had our fun, but even then, we knew that if our defiance was detected, we were certain to face the consequences. And those consequences would not be good ones, especially if my mother was the first to catch us misbehaving! Selma was a small, quiet town. But don't let that fool you. Everyone knew everybody, and no one was a stranger. Any parent in the neighborhood could discipline any child and would report it back to your parent. Once they were informed of your behavior, it was certain you'd be disciplined a second or even a third time, if they pondered over it long enough. So, you had better watch out and be on your best behavior as much as you possibly could.

I was the youngest of three children born to my mother. My birth certificate identified my mother's occupation as a Wash Woman. The delivery doctor was Dr. N. D. Walker, the father of Eunice Walker Johnson. Eunice was also born and raised in Selma. She later married John H. Johnson of Johnson Publishing Company, and she later became famously known as the founder of Ebony Fashion Fair, an extension of Ebony magazine. Ebony was published circa 1945. This was a magazine which was widely read, loved and held in high regard by many black people.

My mother was a lovely hue of brown, tall in stature and beautiful. She was a strong disciplinarian. If there was a stick around and you weren't on your best behavior, I can assure you that you would become acquainted with that stick much sooner than later. But discipline was always done with love. My mother taught us to do what was right and pleasing in the site of God. Raising us without a prominent male model alongside her did not diminish her ability to manage her children. I was baptized by Rev. J.F. Upshaw. I looked up to him because he exuded so many positive qualities. For as far back as I can remember, the one thing that stands out is how Rev. Upshaw always stood up for what he believed in. He would go up against his entire deacon board if necessary. If there was a church issue and Rev. Upshaw had to make a decision which posed opposition from anyone, and he knew his position was right, he would let them know it. He would not back down. And eventually, he would win them over. They respected him, and I respected him. And once they heard his case, it all made sense. I truly admired the Reverend for the way he handled challenging situations.

I never met my father, so I have no description of his physical appearance. My only recollection for a point of reference is the one day something strange happened while I was outside playing with my friends and listening to them talk about their dads.

My aunt was outside with us, and she appeared amused as she observed us playing and chatting. While the other kids talked about their dads, I sat quietly and listened. As if summoned by an inexplicable queue, a funeral procession passed by. I paused to pay my respects to the hearse and the line of cars I observed moving solemnly down the street. My aunt suddenly yelled, "Hey, Freddy! That's your daddy in that casket!" as she pointed toward the procession.

I know why my aunt would cull that moment to make that announcement, and I was taken aback by this sudden revelation. I paused for a moment so that I could digest the words she had just mixed up and poured into my spirit. I was in total shock. My stomach tightened, I couldn't swallow, and my body began to feel warm all over. I felt angry and confused. I ran home to my mother and described my encounter. I had so many questions, but I only asked one...

*Mama, was that really my daddy in that casket?*

I don't know which struck faster, God's lightning during a storm or the sudden strike of my mother's opened hand making contact with the side of my face. I felt the sting the moment my question parted from my lips and entered the atmosphere!

More so than anything, that slap hurt my feelings, and it only generated additional questions. *What really caused my mother to slap me? What transpired between my mom and dad? Was it my fault? Was I merely a byproduct of a circumstance?* I walked around for a very long time with imbedded anger and unanswered questions. But with God's help, the anger subsided over time, and somehow both the hurt and anger disappeared.

My grandmother, Rosa, cooked and cleaned house for Mrs. Julia, a white citizen of Selma. Mrs. Julia was quite fond of my grandmother and would often demonstrate her affection by giving my grandmother food to bring home to us from time to time. Sometimes, it would be enough for an entire meal. Other times, it may have been bread, meat or eggs. There was an unsaid rule in our household which mandated all of the children under the Reese/Sims roof to develop good ethics, good work habits and good study habits. I think we secretly enjoyed the structure in our home. In some cases, it felt as if we were in our own world. There was never confusion or chaos. No home is perfect, but ours was very well run. We had two bedrooms, a kitchen and front and back perches. During the winter months, the house was heated with a wood/coal stove in the front bedroom. The back bedroom was heated by a wood fireplace. On those cold winter nights, I can remember the family gathering around one of these areas and enjoying either the crackling sound of the wood from the fireplace and the sometimes mysterious and dreamy flames which danced from the fire. Our food was cooked in the kitchen on a wood fire stove. Since I was the youngest male in my immediate family, my responsibility was to bring in the wood and coal to be burned in the stove or fireplace during the winter months. I thoroughly enjoyed my duties. It made me feel as though I was in charge of things, and in my mind, instead of being the youngest "man" in the house, I felt like I was THE man in the house! That small duty of responsibility alone gave me so much pride and joy. In my eyes, I was taking charge and taking care of my family.

My uncle William was only three months older than me. Because we grew up together, we were often mistaken for brothers, and we got along like brothers. We laughed, played together, and enjoyed life. We got along sometimes, and sometimes not so much. But we shared so many experiences together, and I had a lot of love for my uncle William.

I have such fond memories of many of the families from Lawrence Street, Selma Avenue and Jeff Davis Avenue, and I must name those families: Smitherman, Mosely, Essie and Babe, Corine, Taylor, Farley, Goldsby, Hill, Hrobowski, Edwards and Miller. The Reese, Farley and Sims families would participate in what we called "dinner saving," where families would share small portions of their dinner with agreed members of the other family. We encouraged and embraced the spirit of sharing. This was a gesture that allowed for "togetherness" during hard times. Some of my favorite people included Paul, Johnny, Margarite,

Mary Louise and Theodore. All were brothers and sisters who resided on Lawrence Street, which was two houses down from where I resided.

Developmental and scholastic learning was expected from my sisters, Rosetta and Annie, and myself. Moreover, that same expectation was placed upon my three uncles: Louis, James and William, and my aunt Mildred, who also lived in the two-bedroom house with my mother and my grandmother, Rosa, completing our household as a family of nine.

The city school law would not allow me to enroll in the first grade at Clark Elementary School until I reached the age of six. Until I reached legal age, I attended the nursery school located on Selma University's campus, where my mother was employed as one of the nursery school teachers. My physical stature and mental development were greater than that of the other five-year-olds enrolled in my class. Nursery school neither stimulated nor challenged me. I was advanced and felt confined since I was more advanced than my classmates. Consequently, my mother met with the principal, Mr. Edwards, and the first-grade teacher, Mrs. Calena Sullivan, and requested that I sit with her first-grade students until I reached the legal age to enroll as a first grader. My mother's request was granted, and I thrived. At the end of the school year, I was promoted to the second grade.

I know that each of my teachers instilled lessons that allowed me to develop character, gifts and qualities that I display to this day. And those are the qualities that I will share with others throughout my lifetime. And for that reason, I must take the time to pay homage to each of those teachers for contributing to my cognitive development as a young boy in Selma's elementary school system. My mother, my upbringing and my education molded me as a man.

Mrs. L.P. Brown, my second-grade teacher, took me by my bootstraps and propelled me to be a good listener.

"Frederick, focus on what I am saying to you. Hold on to my every word. Wait until I finish speaking, then you make a statement or ask a question. This will make you become a great listener."

Mrs. Brown pushed me to go the extra mile with my studies. She reminded me to listen. She was like a football coach. She pushed me to the max. If I appeared to be preoccupied during the time she was teaching, she would stop teaching and ask me if I was listening. Mrs. Brown was also a stickler for good penmanship and great writing skills. Though I was only in the second grade, she told me that she expected the best from me. I wouldn't have understood it then, but as I look back now, I realize that her consistent pressure made a difference. By the end of the school year, she expressed that she could see a positive change in my listening and writing skills. This marked the beginning of my journey as an independent thinker. I was on the right path for academic development.

When I was promoted to the third grade, Mrs. Sanders was my teacher. She picked up where Mrs. Brown left off by placing more emphasis on my writing skills and by introducing me to the art of demonstrating reasoning skills. Incidentally, it was at this time in my life that those around me discovered that I had a festering, uncontrollable temper. My temper caused me to be labeled as "bad." I walked into the classroom each day as if I owned stock in the place. If a boy was bouncing a ball and I wanted it, I took it. If I didn't want to wait in line for something, I broke it. I would disrupt class by talking while Mrs. Sanders was teaching. I wouldn't listen to anyone. I would fight at the drop of a hat, and everyone who knew me knew that I had a major problem with my temper and I had an attitude that was out of this world. Neither guidelines nor regulations applied to me. I, Frederick Reese, was the exception to every rule.

Mrs. Corine Webb was my fourth-grade teacher. She was very gentle in nature and exhibited a motherly, nurturing demeanor toward all of her students. Oftentimes, I would use her meekness to my advantage, and I proceeded to do exactly what I wanted or didn't want to do in her class. If I didn't wish to pay attention, I wouldn't pay attention. If I decided there was someone in class I wanted to talk to, I would spark a conversation, and I couldn't have cared less what Mrs. Webb or anyone else thought about it. In my mind, I was exempt from the rules and regulations of the classroom. I was incorrigible. As a result of my being both stubborn and cavalier, my actions spoke louder than my words. And unfortunately for me, the result of my incessant behavior caused me to miss the mark and fail to achieve the heights of academic progress that I knew I was capable of reaching at the time. With all the potential I possessed, I failed to apply it. I may have let others and myself down, but I didn't care.

Mrs. Quintein Miriam was my fifth-grade teacher. She introduced me to American Literature, and boy did I enjoy it! I took a temporary furlough from my activities of being mischievous and fighting whenever I could. Alternately, I transferred my energy to a subject that captured my undivided attention. I was intrigued by the writings of famous literary giants such as Edgar Allen Poe, Herman Melville, Harriet Beecher Stowe and Emily Dickinson to name just a few. The writings of these geniuses captured my undivided attention and motivated my senses. I definitely felt an intriguing connection. I could read for hours on end. It was through American Literature that I clinched a tremendous amount to knowledge, insight and appreciation. It allowed me to study some great works of the past and push forward to inspire and aspire for a great future.

Mrs. Ernestine Brooks was my sixth-grade homeroom teacher. I took the news of being assigned to her classroom nonchalantly. It was a brand-new school year, but it made no difference to me. I knew I would be reverting to my old ways, and I also knew that misconduct was my best friend. I was a year older, and I was growing bolder! I didn't care what Mrs. Brooks had to say. I was going to be "me." My friends were in my class, and I knew that the fellas and I were going to have a good time. We always had a good time in class. The group of guys I would hang with were just as mischievous as I was, but they would normally follow my lead. If I wasn't playing, I was probably engaging in a fight. When I was fighting, they were watching. I was ready to let the show begin. So I thought. But unfortunately for me, my cavalier approach and plans for resistance to possessing good conduct in the classroom were greeted with a severe reality check quite early. As a matter of fact, I was brought to my senses just a few days after classes began. I had no idea that Mrs. Brooks didn't play!

It was the start of a Wednesday morning. A few of my friends and I started talking loudly and playing around in the back of the classroom. The first time we were too loud, Mrs. Brooks glanced at us and proceeded to talk to two of my classmates regarding last night's homework assignment. We kept walking back and forth, laughing and standing around. The second time she clapped her hands and yelled at us. I glanced at her, but snickered and kept tossing a small ball into the air and catching it. *"Who does she think she is?"* I thought to myself.

"Alright, young men. No horse playing in here. Sit down and be quiet," she said to all of us while making eye contact with only me. My friends briefly stopped playing and returned to their seats. I looked at them, shrugged my shoulders and remained standing. Now, mind you, I'm Fred Reese. *Who did Mrs. Brooks think she was talking to?* I decided to challenge Mrs. Brooks by continuing to talk to my friends, playfully punching them and teasing them, saying that they were scared of Mrs. Brooks. I threw the ball even higher into the air. They laughed and played along as I continued with the shenanigans in the back of the classroom. They played along, but remained seated. I totally ignored Mrs. Brooks' final warning and kept doing what I was doing. Within seconds, it dawned on me that my cohorts were no longer participating and I was playing around by myself. With my back turned from Mrs. Brooks, I saw fear on my friends' faces as they were all trying to communicate with their eyes. Suddenly, I heard the voice of Mrs. Brooks and I could feel the heat of her presence as she was now standing less than an inch behind me. I never turned around, but I veered at her from the corner of my eye. My eyes bounced from the faces of my friends and then back to Mrs. Brooks, who I could still see from my peripheral view. I intently listened while she spoke through clenched teeth, in a stern, matter-of-fact tone, with bursts of heat traveling from her mouth and flowing directly into my left ear. She was mad!

"Frederick Reese. Your mother told me that you are a handful. She also told me that if you misbehaved in my class and if you were not excelling in your subject matter grades, that she would severely apply the correction rod. So, you know what? If you don't straighten up right now, it sounds like you are in store for a major behind whipping." I had no idea that my dear mother had already engaged in a heart to heart with Mrs. Brooks, so I knew I had to straighten up. And the command in Mrs. Brooks' voice roared like that of an army General. The entire class grew silent. Needless to say, after that stern warning, I had no academic challenges and I knew that I could never misbehave in her class again. I sat my behind in my chair, and Mrs. Brooks didn't hear a sound from me the remainder of the school year. But true to the pattern, my good behavior didn't last for too long thereafter, and my antics began to resurface once again.

Mrs. Kathryn Lynn graced the stage as my homeroom teacher in the seventh grade. Mrs. Lynn was quite memorable. My other teachers were memorable also, but Mrs. Lynn holds a special spot in my heart, although you wouldn't know that since my incorrigible behavior managed to spill over into her class just like it had spilled over into all of the others. But Mrs. Lynn was very loving and kind. I can recall the time when my classmate, Timothy, made me mad by kicking the back of my chair. I don't know why he was behaving in this manner, but it wasn't my responsibility to ask why. So, I reached back and grabbed his leg so that he wouldn't entertain a second thought of doing it again. But he did it again, grabbing my leg and then hitting me in the back of the head. I grabbed his arm and yanked it as hard as I could. I jumped out of my chair and I punched him as hard as I could. I snapped. I had a hot temper, and my classmates knew it. They began to scatter across the room because they knew that the gauge on my meter had moved from zero to one thousand in a matter of seconds. I grabbed Timothy, punched him in the face again and flung him across the room like a ragdoll. The girls frantically screamed, and the boys were pumping their fists in the air as they jumped up and down, ecstatic to see a fight. They had all seen me fight before, and they knew that I was about to put on a show. And I was ready to give them one! I had to warm up a bit, so I began moving my arms to simulate one-two punches, upper cuts, jabs and hooks; all while bouncing around in place. After I was satisfied with the pre-show performance, I moved in on Timothy again. My classmates watched in excitement as I beat Timothy to a pulp. You couldn't tell me that I wasn't the boxing great, Joe Lewis. My adrenaline was pumping, and I was still hopping around, asking Timothy if he wanted some more.

I heard a soft voice demanding that I stop. I remember seeing two beautiful hands with well-manicured nails tugging at my shirt. I was still bouncing and flexing when I looked from Timothy, who was sprawled on the floor in pain, and then I looked straight into the eyes of Mrs. Lynn, who was now holding a very big stick! It wasn't long before I felt a sharp, dull pain radiating from my buttocks and up my lower back. I knew Mrs. Lynn kept a big stick and a strap in class, and I also knew that it would be used on anyone who would misbehave, become boisterous or simply fail to follow the rules. But I hadn't imagined she would use either of them on me! I was taught by my mother and by my teachers to be respectful and obedient. Most children were brought up with the same premise. But I didn't feel the rule still applied to me. I was practically grown! But, strike after strike, the stick connected with my body, and I wiggled and writhed with pain during my punishment. The whipping seemed to have hurt Mrs. Lynn more than it hurt me. She cried more than I did as she pulled me to the side and expressed her disappointment in my classroom behavior. While my temper did not soften, I will be the first to admit that it bothered me knowing that I made Mrs. Lynn cry. I will never forget Mrs. Lynn, and I will never forget that whipping!

My eighth-grade year was a challenging one. The challenge was not due to academics. Unfortunately, it was due to my involvement in a freak accident. One day while I was walking around in my neighborhood, I saw a runaway, two-horse drawn wagon bolting down Lawrence Street in front of the family house. I thought I was daydreaming! I looked around to see if anyone was in the area. But there was no one in sight, so I knew I couldn't get help fast enough. I had to do something to stop that wagon, although I didn't know what to do or how I would do it. I decided to run as fast as I could, take a chance and jump on it. After jumping onto the wagon, I staggered and proceeded to looked around, trying to determine my next step. I desperately tried to grasp the reins, but I couldn't reach them. My luck turned for the worse and after several attempts, I failed to grab a hold of it. The wagon seemed to have picked up speed and was now going faster and faster. For the life of me, I was unable to grasp those horse reins. After several unsuccessful attempts, I was forced to jump off the side of the wagon. To my chagrin, my leg landed between the front and back wheels of the wagon, which was still moving. The wagon won the fight when it flipped over and kissed a tree in my neighbor's front yard. I fractured my right leg. The same doctor who delivered me into this world, Dr. N. D. Walker, set my leg bone and fitted me with a cast. I was incapacitated for six weeks. My eighth-grade homeroom teacher, Mrs. Hubbert, offered to assist in any way she could by making sure that I received all of my assignments at home during my six weeks of recuperation. She dropped off my assignments and didn't leave before making sure all of my questions were answered and I had everything I needed. Due to her dedication as an educator and going the extra mile for me, I completed my requirements and I successfully passed the eighth grade.

It was also during my eighth-grade year that I began working for Mr. John Melton, a white man who ran the Western Freight Railroad office. Due to his physical handicap, he required assistance with transporting abstracted freight waybills between three locations. I made daily trips from the Western Railroad freight office, the Western Railroad yard office and the Southern Railroad freight office, all located within the radius of a quarter of a mile. I attended school and I attended every single day. My work hours were from 5:00 p.m. until 11:00 p.m. nightly.

Freight cars would arrive with waybills detailing the enclosed contents. My job was to type the contents of the waybill onto special abstract forms, stamp the forms and then take them to the yard office. Once the freight cars were connected to their assigned freight train, the waybills were used to provide all information once the freight train reached its destination.

I worked at the freight office from grades eight through twelve. While I was waiting to transport waybills to the yard office, I utilized the down time for academic study. I also taught myself how to type by practicing on an old, unused typewriter that was positioned on a table tucked away in the back of the freight office. I became so proficient that Mr. Melton asked me to assist him with the abstracting responsibilities of the job. I worked hard, and I was well aware of my value to the company. After working there for approximately two years, I asked Mr. Melton for a raise, which, coming from a young black boy like myself, was taboo and unheard of during that era. But I wasn't like everyone else. *Closed mouths don't get fed* popped up in my mind. It was a phrase I had often heard, but never understood the depth of its meaning until now. I knew I deserved a raise, and I wasn't afraid to place my cards on the table. I had to speak out. I had to stand up for myself.

"What did you just ask me, boy?" He sneered at me.

Confident, I looked at him, man to man, "I'm requesting a raise, Mr. Melton."

He instantly snapped. I worked with this man on a daily basis and he appeared to be a respectful white man. I had no problems with him prior to this. He had always praised my work, so his behavior caught me by surprise. His tone and demeanor seemed somewhat off balance and out of character. I looked on in astonishment as he reached for a brick which was near the potbelly stove. *I know this man doesn't think I'm going to sit here and allow him to strike me with a brick!* His anger grew, and my eyes were fixated on both him and the brick, which his huge, scruffy fingers were clenching tightly in his left hand.

He erupted, "I'm gonna hit you with this brick for asking me something like that!"

I politely raised from my chair, "Sir, please take back everything I have ever used in this office. The typewriter, the paper, the writing utensils, and anything else I've utilized during my tenure here. Effective immediately, I no longer work for you. I will not stoop to your level of violence. Am I afraid? Yes. I'm afraid that if I feel a breeze from the force of that brick being thrown as close as an inch near me, I will have to lay hands on you. And when I'm finished with you, one of us won't be breathing. And it won't be me."

I stood up, eased my chair back and positioned it back under the desk where I had been working. I headed toward the door. From the corner of my right eye, I could see his bubble of anger deflate. His grip on the brick loosened, and his arm slowly descended to his side, which I interpreted as a sign of defeat. He plopped down in his large wooden chair, and his jaw nearly dropped to the floor. Without looking back, I placed my hand on the door knob and quietly closed the door behind me.

I knew I didn't want any trouble. I no longer had my job, but I walked away beholding a treasure more valuable than a paycheck. I walked away with my pride and dignity. I had progressed so well with my anger issues, and I wasn't allowing this encounter to tarnish what I had worked so hard for. I loved my job, but I refused to work under those conditions. I immediately went to work for Miller's Lumber Company. The work was easy physical labor. This was void of challenge for me. I was great with the physical work, but I preferred a job that tapped into my business acumen. It wasn't long after the day that I walked out of the freight office that Mr. Melton frantically began to reach out to me. He was relentless with sending me letters and extending his deepest apologies. He begged and pleaded for my return to the freight office. His letters expressed that he meant no harm. He would then go on and on, stating that the freight office was not functioning properly because no one could run the office the way I did. I waited a while before deciding to go back. I only returned because the job was fulfilling for me. I enjoyed what I excelled at, and I knew the office ran smoothly because of me. Not boastful. Just facts. I decided that I would allow Mr. Melton to eat a bit more humble pie before I made a move. Eventually, I returned. But I would only return on my terms. I told Mr. Melton that I had to be compensated according to my work ethic and quality of work. I also advised him that he was to treat me with the utmost respect and never threaten me in any way again. He eagerly accepted all of my terms and topped it. He granted me double what I was being paid before and also promised that I would be allowed to work extra hours whenever any of the permanent employees were out on vacation.

Unsurprisingly, my return was not welcomed by those who

had to work directly with me in the freight office. I dealt with blatant expressions of resentment. I ignored the sneers, dirty looks and occasional condescending comments from the whites who came into the office while I was working. I can recall a time when Mr. Melton had left me in charge during his absence and one of the workers needed a signature for a waybill. I advised the worker that I could sign the document. That white man turned beet red and just stared at me. After I repeated that Mr. Melton was not in and that I was authorized to provide a signature, he stared at me for almost thirty seconds until he reconciled with the fact that he had no other choice. He reluctantly threw the waybill on top of the table where I was working. I reviewed the waybill, signed my boss' name, initialed it and politely handed it back to him. Deep down inside, I knew his fury was due to the fact that I was a young black man with exceptional and undeniably in-demand skills at that freight office. In addition to that, I was contained, confident and focused. My work was always accurate, and I always provided my work well ahead of the mandatory deadlines. I knew how to handle business. I knew how to make that office run smoothly, whether Mr. Melton was in the office or away for an extended period of time. The white man's fury didn't frustrate me. No one's fury frustrated me. Instead, it fueled me to take a stand. I was determined to stand out in a positive way and to set an example by paving the way for more opportunities for others, not only young blacks who may come after me, but for all minorities to diversify the workplace. I wanted to make an impact and strive to abolish barriers reviewed for future positions at the freight office. I wanted to leave a mark, and I did. My reputation preceded me at the freight office for years.

Upon entering the ninth grade, I discovered that Mrs. Lovenia Ramsey Brown was my homeroom teacher. She allowed me to think freely and without judgment. She also took the time to sit down with me face to face and discuss my future plans. Together, we sorted out my skills, and she helped me to sort out the things I was most passionate about in order to help determine my academic direction. I realized this was serious business and represented the process of setting a path that would affect the rest of my life. The instruction I received in the areas of Science and Mathematics impacted my future college major and minor course decisions. This was an important school year for me. Science and math were the focal points of my academic mold, and I felt great about it.

Mr. Jerry Montgomery was my English Literature teacher. Similar to my fascination with literature in Mrs. Miriam's class, Mr. Montgomery introduced me to another facet of the subject, and it was through his teachings that I was able to engage and attribute my love and appreciation for it. Mr. Montgomery encouraged each of his students to exercise the liberty of interjecting our personal interpretation sans judgment. He also welcomed our thoughts and views. And for me, that was like taking a breath of fresh air. It made me feel free, and I loved freedom. My love for literature as a whole was one of the few things that positively preoccupied my mind.

My uncontrollable temper was displayed in many of my everyday dealings. Anger was a vice that dominated my life. As some might say, *I didn't even play the radio*. I can remember one day as I was going to the store, a boy in the neighborhood said something to me that I didn't like. Asking questions was neither a priority nor a necessity when I felt I was being challenged, let alone confronted. So, no questions asked, I went in on this boy with both hands and both feet. I wanted to break every bone in his body. I fought him as if my life depended on it. After I'd had enough, and knew that I had punched him enough, I got off of him. Though slightly disheveled and winded, I was satisfied with my boxing match. I proudly dusted myself off and continued to the store to pick up the items I was sent to retrieve before I was so rudely interrupted.

That incidence of distraction surreptitiously marked my last round of violence and final display of extreme temperament. I never started a fight, but I would never back down or run from one either. So, unbeknownst to me, my life was about to make an unprecedented 180-degree turn. No one could have convinced me that my propensity for violence would be superseded by diplomacy and reasoning. And even if they would have tried, I would have advised them that they were wasting their time.

So, the following day, I proceeded with my usual routine. Nothing changed. Nothing felt differently. I got up, got dressed and walked to school. I entered my homeroom and talked to a few of my classmates, joked around and engaged in thoughtless chatter until our lesson began. Our school did not provide our meals, nor did we have a cafeteria. So, students were required to bring lunch from home. Lunch and recess times were combined, so when the designated time arrived, our teacher would announce the class break. All of the kids would eagerly grab their lunches and run out the door and over to the designated area to eat and then proceed to the playground. My family was poor. The majority of my classmates' families were poor, but some of the children's lunches contained more food than others. My mom couldn't afford to send me to school with a hearty meal. But that didn't bother me because I enjoyed eating the baked sweet potato that was packed for me each and every day. A baked sweet potato. Every single day. It became a bit monotonous at times, but a "stomach full is a stomach full." She also taught me to be grateful for what we had, no matter how it compared to others. And grateful I was.

So, that day I ate my baked sweet potato and headed to the Downing Ground. The Downing Ground was a designated area on the playground where all the boys would gather around for the dozens game and horseplay. The rule of the Downing Ground was when a boy stood in the marked section of the playground, he could be challenged by any other boy to be boxed or wrestled down to the ground. Hence the name Downing Ground. Everyone looked forward to going to the Downing Ground. Sometimes, it was the highlight of the entire school day. I loved the adrenaline rush I felt when I would go in, get ready for the challenge and wrestle my opponent to the ground. I was well-known for my fighting skills. Everyone knew I was a leading contender.

Well, the moment I stepped into the designated area that day, without one single word, a boy briskly walked up to me. Open-handed, with a fierce look in his eyes, he landed a forceful slap across the left side of my face! When he struck me, it felt like an electrical shock. The cacophonous impact resounded in all sections of the playground. All of my friends were aware that I had a violent temper, so they immediately gathered closer and began calling others over to observe. I heard comments like, "Uh, oh! That boy's gonna get it!" "C'mon everybody. This is going to be a good fight." "Freddy is angry!"

But anger was far from what I was feeling at that time. Instead, I suddenly felt a wave of calm. At that moment in time, I experienced an epiphany. All of the past rage and anger that used to consume me and reside within my core was no longer present. I could hear a voice whispering to me, "When are you going to control your temper?" The message was so vivid that I had to stop and ask myself, *When am I going to control my temper?* That moment was both powerful and cathartic. I slowly stepped out of the circle and walked past my friends and the onlookers. Even the boy who slapped me just stood there and observed as I made my unprecedented journey to the principal's office to report the incident. While reporting that slap, I acquiesced to a pivotal moment. For the first time in my life, I had exercised control over my temper, and what a monumental day that was. I now had restraint over my emotions. I did not know at that time that God was using me and preparing me to lead a nonviolent movement 20 years later in Selma/Dallas County, Alabama. It was then that I embraced the idea that the measure of a man or woman is not determined by how much you can give, but by how much you can take. From that day forward, I've never lost my temper again.

During my eleventh-grade academic experience, Mrs. Gracie DeYampert was very encouraging as a homeroom and literature instructor. Literature continued to be the motivating force behind my love for the subject. It dominated my overall interests, and I thoroughly enjoyed the style in which she presented the material. I was also intrigued by Mr. John Shields, another one of my eleventh-grade teachers, who introduced me to his knowledge and passion for American History. It was at this point that I first learned about Christopher Columbus, The Stamp Act, The Bill of Rights, The American Civil War and the many other components that shaped our America.

As a twelfth-grade senior, I wanted the year flow similarly by way of the political process, so to speak. I had been elected as President of the 10th and 11th grade Marshal Patrol. I policed the grounds of the high school since we did not have a fence surrounding the school. I took pride in my role, and I hoped my 12th grade year would give way to greater responsibilities and more opportunities. I knew early on that I wanted to be the change and create a change. I also wanted to "right" all of the "wrongs" I could. And I felt that becoming a member of the YMCA was a positive addition to my resume and that I was definitely moving a step in the right direction. The more I studied, the more intrigued with the world and life I became, and the more involved I became.

My homeroom teacher was Mr. A.J. Durgan. Mr. Durgan inspired me for the next three years and beyond. I had no idea this man would play such an important role in my achievement of academic excellence. As a tenth grader in biology, an eleventh grader in chemistry and a twelfth grader in physics, I excelled profoundly. My grades were at the top of my class. Mr. Durgan and the teaching staff were collectively proud of my accomplishments. They were also proud of my impressive and distinctive handwriting. I received numerous compliments whenever I presented a paper or passed along a handwritten note. I was constantly amazed at the feedback I received from the way my hand and pen met, gliding across the pages, creating a palette of beautiful numeric and alphabetic artwork. I attribute my great penmanship to the influence of Mr. Durgan during my early years of innocence. That influence continues to flow in my present juncture of life.

I maintained excellent time management skills and a great life/school balance throughout my junior and senior years in high school. I attribute that success to everything I learned while working at the railroad. My desire to be successful also groomed me to maintain an appreciation for punctuality. I've continued to maintain those principles, and I am proud to say they have allowed me to carry a high regard for responsibilities and prompt arrival for engagements to the present day. I graduated high school in 1947.

After gaining four years of experience with Mr. John Melton at the Western Railroad yard, I became eligible for full-time hire. Mr. J.J. Rimes, one of the managers in charge, offered me the position. While excited for the opportunity, I refused the offer. I had decided on a more scholastic path and enrolled as a freshman at Alabama State University in Montgomery, Alabama. My goal was to pursue a major in biology and a minor in mathematics, ultimately landing a career in medicine. That plight was short-lived, due exclusively to a lack of financial resources. So, instead I chose to follow a career path as an educator with a science major and mathematics minor.

My freshman year at Alabama State University was both exciting and adventurous. I resided on Hardaway Street with a family my Aunt Mildred knew. She reached out to them prior to my arrival in town, and her goal for my stay with them was to assist me with "testing the water" before officially venturing out and living on my own. Mildred was a cheerleader of sorts, that charismatic, always supportive auntie who wanted the best for me and who made provisions for me to soar. And I loved her for that.

My new family took me in, and their hospitality generated a "hometown" feel. Aunt Mildred had spoken highly of my host family, and they did not disappoint. They were nice and welcoming. I enjoyed living with them, but after a short period of time, I felt the need to search for another place of my choice. I can't explain it, but while I appreciated my aunt arranging my stay with the Joneses, something inside spoke to me, and I decided to make a change. A few months later, I discovered there was a vacancy down the street at Mrs. Mary Benson's boarding house. I thanked my Aunt Mildred and I thanked the Joneses. Then I moved out. Benson's Boarding House was a large, well-kept residence with three bedrooms and two bathrooms. Mrs. Benson slept in the back bedroom, and she rented out the two bedrooms that were located in the front of the house. I thoroughly enjoyed my stay with Mrs. Benson. We developed a close mother-son relationship. Her warmth and kindness meant a lot to me. We had long talks, and she was quite nurturing. I respected her immensely and grew to love her and the many qualities she possessed.

During my sophomore year, I moved out of the boarding house with Mrs. Benson and into Trenholm Hall, the boy's dormitory located on the Alabama State campus. I enjoyed the camaraderie among my roommates and classmates. College life for me was socially, intellectually and fundamentally rewarding.

My typing experience at the railroad made me a hot commodity while I was in college. I worked odd jobs and utilized a number of my skills. I was in high demand and was hired for cutting stencils and writing term papers and announcements for my roommates and other dormitory occupants. I was paid good money for my on-demand services. I used the money to purchase peanut butter, jelly and light bread on the weekends when the cafeteria was closed during supper time.

During my freshman and sophomore academic years, I successfully maintained a B average nearly every quarter. I had a pretty good voice and I loved to sing, so it was an honor to be accepted as a bass singer with the Alabama State College Traveling Choir, where Dr. Frederick D. Hall was the director. We traveled to various places and sang our hearts out. When no one else in the bass section was able to travel to engagements, Dr. Hall could count on my being there, and I cherished every moment. I can attribute a substantial amount of my subdued temper to my zeal for singing with the choir. I attribute the choir to helping calm and sustain my temper, a vice which once dominated so many aspects of my life.

Toward the end of my sophomore year, I was absorbed with positive social activities. I was elected President of the College Choir. What a joy to be fulfilled and surrounded by great voices and music. I was also President of the Gamma Beta Chapter of the Phi Beta Sigma Fraternity, Inc., my well-loved organization, filled with community service and brotherhood. Subsequently, I was elected President of the Pan Hellenic Council. This organization consumed an enormous amount of my leadership time during my junior year. Unfortunately, as a result of my expanding agenda, I found myself devoting less time to my science and mathematics classes. To my disappointment, my grade average dropped, and I had to make up for classes or repeat some altogether.

My senior year in college greeted me with the difficult challenge of time management. I worked as a janitor at the Wilby and Walton theatre in Selma during the summer. By no means was I a stranger to hard work, but due to unusually taxing classes and long work hours, I struggled with going to school and working. At times, I would work a double shift. I would sleep in a chair for an hour or so, waking up just in time to make it to my next class on time. But it was something I absolutely had to do. My mother was a hard worker as well. She taught me about work ethics. I knew I had to make the same sacrifices I observed by her example. She especially worked hard to make ends meet during my last year, which seemed to be the most challenging. But with God's help, we made it through. She was able to pay my tuition in full, and I was successful in meeting all of my academic requirements. I joined the ranks with my fellow classmates as a proud, distinctive representative of Alabama State University's Graduating Class of May 1951. And the most wonderful feeling was seeing the smile on my mother's face and the joy we both felt when she hugged and kissed me on that day!

# HUSBAND, EDUCATOR, FATHER

" *B*ut as for you, O man of God, flee these things.
Pursue righteousness, godliness, faith, love,
steadfastness, gentleness."

1 Timothy 6:11 (KJV)

I married Alline Toulas Crossing on Sunday, June 28, 1953, at
her grandparents' house in Tennessee. It seems like yesterday,
and it was one of the happiest days of my life. We were twice
blessed, because at the time we exchanged our wedding vows,
my beautiful Alline was radiant and glowing as she was carrying
our first child, Frederick Reese, Jr., in her precious belly. So,
during the '50s, the mere thought of conceiving a child out of
wedlock was a "whispered discussion," especially in a small town
like Selma. And more so since both Alline and I were reared
from families with deeply rooted, devout Christian values.
Nonetheless, we professed our love for God and the love that we
felt for each other. And there were no uncertainties in reference
to whether or not our love was meant to be. If anyone possessed
a negative thought about our love or our lives, it was none of our

business. "Therefore, what God has joined together, let no man put asunder." (Mark 10:9). The only thing that mattered to us was "us" and the start of our new life together ... as a family. As "one." God was, is and always will be the head of our household and the head of our lives. We gravitated toward the things that were important in life. I knew that Alline and I were stitched together, blended and bonded by the beauty of God's favor. We knew that above all, God loved us, and He would not turn His back on us for being the focus of a "whispered discussion." And ultimately, He was the only one who could truly judge us. End of story.

Alline had worked successfully as a school teacher throughout her previous years, and a great teacher she was. She embraced her students as if she had given birth to them naturally. She was warm, but stern. She made sure every student learned the material she was teaching, and she encouraged every student organically: one on one, step by step. And the moment any student seemed to struggle with comprehending the lesson, she would make every effort to bridge that gap. Alline made the phrase "practice makes perfect" an understatement, as she insisted upon breaking through any learning barriers and concentrating on the basics. Alline instilled the importance of education in her classroom, and she was blessed with the ability to teach with clarity. What a great gift.

During the timespan of her teaching career, Alline would often tell me about the quality time she spent with her students. While listening to Alline, it warmed my heart to see the twinkle in her eyes and hear the soothing melodies in her tone as she described interactions with her students. She often shared some of the comical outtakes from the classroom as well as some of the more poignant moments, such as innocent playtime or a student who cried because he or she felt the class work was impossible to achieve or complete. The students would be filled with so much joy when they realized they had conquered their struggle. Aiding students in successfully jumping over hurdles was another forte in Alline's list of "know-hows." I was proud to see first-hand how much Alline made a difference in the lives of her students as well as the staff at Wilcox Training School. To be completely honest, my Alline made a difference in the community, her church and everywhere she stepped foot. She was and still is well respected by many residents of Selma. To many of her students, Alline was a mother figure. To her colleagues, she was a role model. And to many others, she's still simply a sweet woman. To me, she's my world.

Alline and I were covered in marital bliss. From the first time she sashayed into our kitchen, working her magic hands, she spoiled me with the most delectable meals one could imagine. I thank God that the love of my life is a culinary genius. I awoke each day to a five-star breakfast, consisting of a mouth-watering stack of buttered flapjacks, golden eggs over-easy, creamy, hot buttered grits, a savory country sausage and topping it off with the beverage of my choice. Every Thursday, she prepared greens, baked chicken, liver and rice. For lunch, I would enjoy hot links, and later in our marriage, I would eat a midnight snack from the Colonel himself, also known as KFC and Kentucky Fried Chicken!

Though Alline made a tremendous impact as an educator and mentor to the students, together we decided to turn the page and begin a new chapter. Now that she had become "Mrs. Reese" and was about to become the mother of our child, we decided that she would extend her well wishes to the students and faculty as she would no longer remain at Wilcox Training School. Instead, she would take on a brand-new role as a full-time wife and mother. Neither of us could have been happier, as we both agreed upon and loved the idea!

I learned early on, from the days of bringing in wood for the fireplace and taking on household chores in the role of "man of the house," that my heart's desire was to create the best atmosphere for my family and provide for them in the best way I knew how. I was proud of the man I was becoming, and Alline basked in realizing the woman she was blossoming into. Wow! We were not only growing as man and woman, but we were flourishing as husband and wife. And now, we were ecstatic as soon-to-be parents. Our blessings and our cup were running over! Isn't God good? *

Alline's contractions began all of a sudden. We knew the baby would be coming any day, but as first-time parents, we weren't sure what to expect. But as soon as Alline gave the word, we headed to the hospital. The drive to the hospital was filled with both apprehension and excitement. Apprehension because of the unknown, and excitement due to our welcoming a new life into the world. Alline remained relatively calm, and I managed to keep my emotions under control as well. I must say we made a great team. I kept both hands on the steering wheel until Alline felt a contraction. At that time, I would extend my hand so that she could hold it and squeeze as necessary. I kept asking her if she was okay. I could hear her taking deep breaths, and then she would reply with a comforting, "I'm okay." When we arrived at the hospital, I opened the door, pulled the key out of the ignition, exited the car and closed the door. I ran around the front of the car and after I grabbed the door handle, I carefully guided Alline out of the vehicle. Never taking my eyes off her, I rushed Alline inside the hospital door and I checked her in. After waiting about fifteen minutes, Alline was finally called by the receptionist and taken to the back. I told Alline that I would be patiently waiting and that everything would be fine. I could hear the voices and the footsteps of the medical personnel as they took Alline to the back room. The sound of the voices trailed off and I heard the door close loudly behind them. I imagine my nerves must have begun to set in because I felt the need to stand up. I must have walked back and forth the length of the waiting area ten times before I decided I should sit and wait until I heard word from the doctor. And that, I did. I waited. I waited. And I waited. I'm not certain how many people were in the room with me, or if there were any at all. My focus was on Alline and the baby. I noticed a magazine on the end table next to the door of the waiting area, and as I reached down to pick it up, a small bible appeared right below it, so I began reading God's word.

Sometime later, I could hear muffled sounds coming from the room Alline had been taken to, but nothing more. I checked my watch, I read a few more scriptures, I sang to myself, I prayed. Then I waited some more. I stood still, tilted my head and tried to listen out for any indication of what may have been taking place. Nothing. I prayed and I waited. Nothing. Finally, as more time passed, it was if someone turned up the volume behind the delivery room door. Eventually, I heard, "We're almost there! I can see the baby's head. Push! One more time! Push! Wait, b-r-e-a-t-h-e.... You're doing a great job!" My heart was racing as I waited patiently, yet nervously in the waiting area. I had faith that everything would be fine, but for some reason, I couldn't help but feel anxious. My thoughts were inundated and I was flushed with a stream of emotions. I felt helpless, so all I knew to do was pray:

*Lord, please cover Alline with grace and mercy. Bless this birth and bless us with a healthy baby. Allow your anointing to move throughout this entire building and through the hands of those who are delivering our baby. I ask these and many more blessings in your mighty and precious name. Amen.*

"That's it! Take a deep breath. And when I say, "NOW," I need you to push with all of your might. Okay? You're doing great, Alline. Breathe in through your nose, taking a deep breath and then, hold it. When I tell you to, I want you to push..... *Now, puuuush*! That's it. Puuuush! Keep pushing. Don't stop! Okay. Breathe... You can relax. After that, I didn't hear a sound. *What's going on?* I thought to myself. "One last push, Alline. NOW!" Before my body could go into full panic mode, I too, took a deep breath. Following my inhale of air, breaking its way through the atmosphere was the most angelic sound my ears had ever heard. The precious sound of our baby's first cry sent melodic sound waves throughout the door, up the hallway and straight to my soul. "You may come to the back now, Mr. Reese." The unidentified staff member directed me toward the labor room door and walked away. Pausing to gain my composure, I adjusted my tie, swept my hand downward to smooth out my crisp, white shirt and dusted myself off. I was as clean as a whistle, but I wanted to look my best when I reunited with my wife and met my baby for the very first time. So, I exhaled and gently placed my hand on the door, slowly turning the knob. As I walked in, I saw Alline holding my name sake, Frederick D. Reese Jr. She was smiling and caressing his precious little face. I briefly closed my eyes and thanked the Lord for what He had just done. "Take a look at your handsome son," Alline chimed. I leaned over to kiss both Alline and our tiny bundle of joy. Alline appeared exhausted, but she was glowing more now than ever while cradling our precious gift. At that moment, we prayed together, for the first time with our new addition. Alline and I thanked God for allowing us to be the proud parents of this beautiful baby boy. Together, we counted ten tiny fingers and ten tiny toes. We couldn't have been happier!

Life in the Reese household moved along smoothly. I provided for my family financially and took care of the upkeep of the outside. I spent a great deal of time on the road, lending a voice and spreading the importance of fighting against the disenfranchisement of voting rights and speaking at various venues to bring awareness to voting rights and their importance whenever

I could. Meanwhile, Alline took care of the essentials, mothered our son and took great care of everything inside of the home. Alline never reflected upon the length of time I spent away from our family. She always expressed to me that she was aware there was work to be done. She knew that I was called to do the type of work I was so passionate and determined to continue. My work and my calling were the forces that propelled me to continuously take a stand for the injustices in Selma. Alline was and remains strong emotionally, and she was unconditionally supportive throughout all of my endeavors. She never questioned my passion nor doubted my intention. Equally and lovingly noted, she never complained. Her genteel spirit never ceased to amaze me.

We attended church every Sunday. Our house was always tidy and in order. Alline had always been the apple of my eye, and still is. I would look at her and smile during church service as she held Frederick Jr. God had blessed me with a beautiful family. I was truly happy, and my life was great. But life in the Reese family was about to make a turn for the worse after we heard the heartbreaking news.

Frederick Jr. was approximately 2 years old when the doctor looked Alline and I directly in the eyes and told us that my namesake, our pride and joy and our only child, had muscular dystrophy. Neither of us expected to hear such devastating news. Frederick Jr. didn't seem to be as physically active as other children his age, but his mental capacity was sharp. He would play, smile and laugh to his heart's content. He was such a loving child. To us, he was otherwise happy. Alline fed him, kept him clean and took great care of him. He was a healthy child, or so we thought. We didn't know much at all about the disease, and we looked to the doctor for guidance and understanding.

The doctor informed us that muscular dystrophy is a disease that would initially affect Fred Jr.'s muscles and his ability to walk. The portion of the doctor's conversation that broke our hearts the most was when he explained that there is no cure for muscular dystrophy, and as the disease progressed, Fred. Jr. would develop heart and breathing complications, and that we should prepare to lose him between his teenage years and his early 20s. *My God, My God.* Alline and I looked at each other. I could see the pain in her eyes, and I could feel a sense of heaviness throughout my entire body. I had to be strong for her, but I felt like a small part of me had just been taken away. Alline opened her mouth to speak, but she was at a loss for words. So, I held her and she leaned her head on my shoulder as we sat side by side in silence. The doctor provided us with additional information and answered any questions which remained. He apologized for Fred Jr.'s prognosis and left us alone to digest the news.

After we arrived back home, Alline and I talked and prayed. Neither of us could keep our eyes off of Fred Jr. He would look at us and smile. We would smile back. It was difficult knowing that behind his cute little smile were innocence and sincerity, but behind our smiles were sadness and uncertainty. Our faith in God never wavered, but we're human. We didn't question God, but we were hurting. We relied on Him for strength, because if we never needed Him before, we definitely needed Him then. Alline and I agreed that we wanted Fred Jr. to lead a normal life as much as possible. We would trust God to get us through, and

He had never let us down before. Alline made it clear that my mission would continue and she would take care of Fred Jr.

I knew that the Reese household would stand in spite of our circumstances. Though it seemed that our backs were up against a wall, we had to rely on the Almighty to be a present help in the time of our storm.

～

By mid-1961, Alline was glowing and growing once again. We were expecting our second child, Valerie, and we couldn't have been happier. By this time, Fred Jr.'s condition was under control, and despite our knowledge that he had such a dismal disease, he was fulfilling the hope his mother and I had for him, which was to live a relatively normal life. He attended school each day, and he had lots of friends.

After our precious Valerie was born, she added more joy to our household. She was beautiful, vibrant and filled with spark! And she loved her big brother. Three years later, our son Marvin was born. Our house was filling up fast, and we loved hearing the patter of little feet running around in the house. As Valerie and Marvin grew older, they both helped with Fred Jr.'s care. Marvin helped him with baths, putting on his clothes and getting him ready for bed at night. There were so many hugs and so much love in our home. Everyone in the Reese household could especially benefit from the hugs and love during this time, because after our youngest daughter, Christa, was born in 1968, Fred Jr.'s condition took a turn for the worse. He had reached the age of 15 and no longer had mobility in his legs. Alline and I were apprehensive when the doctor informed us how the disease would progress, but we continued to hope and pray for the most positive outcome. Our family outings no longer included Fred Jr. He could not be left alone because he was unable to walk. As a family, we had to arrange our schedules so that someone could always be at the house with him. He could still laugh and talk, and by the grace of God, Fred Jr. never complained. Marvin spent a tremendous amount of time with his brother. He made sure that after Alline prepared our meal, Fred Jr. received his plate immediately. Marvin embraced the role as Fred Jr.'s caregiver, or his "brother's keeper." Either way, he was committed to comfort and care for his brother in such a way that one's heart would melt. I could look at Marvin sometimes and sense his hurt over his brother's condition, but he remained extremely strong for his brother...he, too, never complained, and he always kept pressing forward.

Alline and I exchanged small talk as we drove from our home en route to one of her doctor appointments. After exiting the car, I walked around and opened the door for Alline. She thanked me and smiled, and we walked into the office. As soon as Alline entered the room, she made a bee line toward the "black" section of the lobby. As I observed her walking ahead of me, I thought, *I've had enough of the division and exclusion. When will this stop? When will blacks be treated as equal and no longer be treated as second-class citizens?* I refused to remain silent. I knew I had to stand up and represent my wife and anyone else subjected to unfair treatment. I politely called my wife's name and gently explained to her that we would not be sitting in the "black" section. I informed her that today and from now on, we would be sitting right up front with the whites. I waited while Alline sat down, and I proudly sat down right beside her. As I expected, when we sat in the "white section," the atmosphere became as cold as ice. You could cut the tension in the room with a knife. We heard gasps, received numerous stares and heard whispering among the whites, who were now staring at Alline and me as if we each had two heads. The receptionist stood and looked at us with a bewildered expression on her face. Then, she immediately sat back down. We were early for our appointment, but I knew that was not the motivation behind her reaction. I imagine that everyone in that room knew that I meant business, and they could tell that I was far from playing games, because the "black section" was clearly marked, and without question, we weren't white. Though it was discernible that the entire room objected to my stance, no one uttered a direct word to either myself or Alline. And had they injected my space with a single word, I was verbally equipped to give them a piece of my mind. So, I looked over at Alline and gave her an assuring, closed-mouth smile. Just as I was about to strike up a conversation with Alline, the receptionist came over and informed us that the doctor was ready to see Alline. Clandestinely amused, I stood as Alline followed the receptionist to the back room. I'm certain that Alline was summoned to see the doctor as soon as possible to avoid a confrontation. I think we broke a record for the shortest "black wait time" in a white doctor's office because Alline was called to see the doctor after about three minutes of joining the white section. A point was made, and a small victory was won.

I knew that the fight was far from over, and there would be additional obstacles to encounter. Lo and behold, we had another doctor visit a short time thereafter, and this time I took issue with how Alline was referenced. From the moment we entered the doctor's office, I observed the receptionist address each female patient as "Mrs." or "Miss." When it was Alline's turn to be called, she simply called her *Alline*. I was appalled. *"Excuse me, ma'am. Every woman you have called prior to calling my wife, regardless of their age, you have addressed them in a formal manner, using "Mrs." or "Miss."* I gently placed my hand on Alline's arm and made an announcement for everyone to hear. *"This is my wife, Mrs. Reese. I repeat, Mrs. Reese. And that's exactly how she is to be addressed in this office. She will be respected and referenced accordingly. Do I make myself clear?"* The room was silent, except for the voice of the receptionist, who nervously began to speak, "Mrs. Reese, the doctor will see you now. Please follow me."

As educators, Alline and I stressed to our children that education was beyond important. They were aware that exceptional grades were expected. End of story. They were also aware that good behavior was a must. While this book was being written, Marvin Sr. openly discussed how he felt when the KKK came around our house in robes. He was also in the next room when the FBI stood in my living room and informed me that there was a hit on my life. Marvin later expressed that after hearing about the hit, he just knew his life was over. He was frightened out of his mind. I had no fear. When the FBI exited my home, I continued doing whatever I was doing prior to their arrival. Alline did the same. We had no fear. I could still be seen marching and protesting an hour, a day or a week from then. I told my children that the KKK was a disgrace to the human race. I knew that my children were forced to share me with the church and the movement. They knew I loved them, and they also knew the importance of the movement, and it was a sacrifice which had to be made.

So, back to Marvin Sr. ... He knew that the only time he would NOT get a whipping as a child was on his birthday. I concur. He also expressed that while everyone around Selma saw his dad as soft-spoken, yet firm and fair, he views me from a different perspective. Marvin Sr. seems to feel that I released all of the self-restraint and furor onto him during his whippings! Well, Marvin Sr. shouldn't have been so mischievous at times! He, too, admitted that he was "all boy." I say that with love, because I must thank God for wonderful children. All of my children are musically inclined, either vocally or via musical instrument. All of my children are anointed with amazing voices; Valerie and Christa play the piano. Many may not know this, but I play the piano as well! Marvin Sr. played the trumpet. To this day, they use their talents through ministry as they touch the lives of others in a mighty way!

Christa, with a talent for writing and poetry, is active in ministry and shares her experience as a child growing up:

"I enjoyed growing up as a preacher's daughter and the child of a civil rights leader. Dad was my school principal in the 7th and 8th grade. As a preacher's daughter, I did not feel any pressure. The

only pressure I felt was the pressure of doing well
academically. I knew I had to be on my best behavior
at all times since my Dad was the principal."

Our youngest son, Alan, was born in 1971. Alline continued to
manage a husband, a newborn, four children and our household
without incident. We leaned on God and each other for strength.
We supported one another mentally and spiritually. The care
of Fred Jr. had become more challenging as his condition was
rapidly changing for the worse. He now required assistance
walking, eating and going to the restroom. He was bedridden
and was in extreme pain. His care required love and patience,
and Marvin was constantly at his brother's side, attending to him
from head to toe.

In 1973, when Alan was 2 years of age, the doctor informed
us that he, too, had muscular dystrophy. Upon hearing the same
news we'd heard nearly 14 years ago, the turn of events seemed
surreal. *How much, Lord? How much pain can we bear?* Our life
was changing once again, and holding on to our faith was all we
could do. But the darkest cloud appeared over our lives on the
day that Marvin, who was only 9 years old at the time, went into
the room to check on his big brother but couldn't awaken him.
Fred Jr. had gone home to be with the Lord. Marvin talks about
that day, as he remembers nearly every detail. He ran into the
kitchen, where his mother had dinner prepared and was then
sitting at the sewing machine. *"Mom! Mom! Fred won't wake up!"*
When he gave her the news, she continued sewing and made no
indication that she had heard Marvin's cry of distress. Perhaps

she couldn't accept the reality that Fred Jr. was gone. Perhaps she wanted to delay the moment she would have to face reality.

Words can't express our sorrow in burying our oldest son, and caring for our youngest son, diagnosed with the same disease and the same prognosis. There are no words to describe our sorrow. No words at all.

Marvin, Valerie and Christa kept up with their chores, homework and the care of Alan, just as they had for Fred Jr. They were extremely loving toward their brother, and all three remained good students in school. I must say, they were all well-rounded. Though I commend them, I wouldn't have had it any other way. I maintained a strict household, and everyone did what they were expected to do.

I had served as pastor of Ebenezer since I accepted the call on March 21, 1965, the same day the Selma to Montgomery march began. The past 19 years at Ebenezer has been remarkable. I had wonderful members, and there was a requited love between my church, my family and I. Upon Frederick Jr.'s passing, the church and the community as a whole extended an enormous amount of love and support, for which I am extremely grateful. We serve an awesome God, for He placed me in an amazing edifice to preach His word. To God be the glory!

I had declared that I would run for City Council again, and the time finally arrived. As time moved forward, I could see that there was a moderate speed to the changes. Though not as swift as I would have liked, it was definitely emerging. During my first run for City Council, my sense of reality allowed me to accept the fact that my chances of victory were fairly slim. However, with this run, I believed my chances were greater. Truthfully, I felt that my time had come, and my faith allowed me to visualize my well-deserved position on the City Council. I ran and I won. One of my first items was changing Sylvan Street to Martin Luther King Street. Initially, I received pushback, because some whites announced their refusal to allow their businesses to be associated with a street named after a black man. Eventually, it was approved, and the street name was changed. I spoke with the residents and voiced my concerns for improved living conditions via new construction within the Felix Heights and surrounding areas. The new buildings eliminated the eyesores and provided more quality-filled living for neighboring residents. Another item implemented was the ban on smoking in City Council Chambers. I was appointed Chairman of the City Street Committee of Selma, where I was successful in improving the conditions of some of Selma's paved streets. I was instrumental in adding a black man to the police force and a black deputy within the Sheriff's department. Not only were they black, but they were the first black men to hold those respective positions. There were several neighborhoods in Selma that required my attention due to the number of elderly living in deplorable conditions. Upon visiting the areas, I could not accept the idea that those who had lived through the difficult times of the past were being forced to live in substandard living quarters. I was instrumental in fighting for the improved buildings, which were erected on Franklin Street in Selma. The units were accommodating and a definite upgrade from the units many elderly were forced to live in prior to my service and representation of their concerns. Also implemented were programs that provided food and transport to doctor's appointments, errands, etc. For the purposes of beautification, serenity and relaxation, we also fought for a park to be created in an area along Voeglin Avenue. It is incumbent upon all of us to take care of our precious gems in the elderly. They are the foundation on which we were raised, and we must build a foundation of happiness for their enjoyment in their golden years. I was proud of my contributions while serving on the Selma City Council. My job duties seemed more of a privilege, as I was serving in the capacity of my calling from God. And in all things, I give Him the honor, the praise and the glory.

In 1984, I announced my decision to run against incumbent Joe Smitherman for the seat of Mayor of Selma. Our town was experiencing a surge in the number of black registered voters, and this seemed to cause concern for the white voters, as they appeared to fear the potential power of the black vote. James Perkins, Jr. served as my campaign manager. Ironically, James' father, James Perkins, Sr., served as my campaign manager when I ran for City Council years ago.

J.L. Chestnut, James Perkins, Jr. and I sat down to discuss and devise my campaign strategy. Immediately, I detected a vast amount of disconnect from J.L. Chestnut and his thought process. J.L. Chestnut suggested that we utilize the race card as a tactic to solidify the white vote. It was not my desire to launch my campaign with a blatant racial agenda. Ironically, Rev. Jesse Jackson came to Selma frequently, as he was campaigning for President of the United States. This was an exciting time. The possibility of a black president created quite a buzz. There was an enormous amount of hope and excitement. As with all elections, there were many who opposed his potential run. Jesse Jackson spent a short time in Selma, and along with campaigning for himself, there was a time when he also campaigned for me.

I attended a heated platform during an interview with the local newspaper regarding my agenda. The paper wanted to hear my take on city jobs. I was bombarded with comments indicating that I planned to fire all whites who currently hold positions and replace them with blacks. Upon attempting to delineate my projected goal and balance of power in a 50/50 split, the meeting became more intense, and the atmosphere more aggressive. I was taken aback by the lack of respect. I pounded on the podium and stated my case. I straightened my tie and walked away. While I continued to maintain the direction originally mapped, unfortunately I was not successful in acquiring the seat as mayor of Selma. I thank James Perkins, Jr. for his dedication and hard work with the campaign. I wasn't alone with my campaign loss. Unfortunately, Jesse Jackson lost his run for President as well. James Perkins, Jr. later ran for mayor in 2000 and won. He became the first black mayor of Selma! I retired as pastor of Ebenezer Baptist church in 2015 after 50 years of service. I passed the baton to James Perkins, Jr. as my successor. My political career and pastorship evolved full circle with James Perkins, Jr. My prayer is that Ebenezer thrives and continues to win souls for Christ.

My loss in the run for mayor did not halt or hinder my drive for fighting injustices. It merely allowed time for me to tackle the future injustices and disparities that awaited me. And immediately, I felt a great deal of concern upon frequenting my local Walmart. As I walked throughout the store, back and forth in the aisles and through each department, I noticed the absence of black managers. On my next trip to the store, the scenario was repeated. I was disturbed to discover that Walmart did not have any blacks in management positions. I was not satisfied with the idea that not one single black person qualified for a position on that level. I asked one of the clerks and I asked to speak with a manager. Both confirmed that the store did not have a black manager. I immediately put my thoughts into action. I decided that one of Walmart's busiest days was rapidly approaching. I would reach out to everyone in the neighborhood and surrounding areas of Selma and arrange a boycott on the 4th of July! If I wanted to be heard, I would need to generate attention when the store had a steady and large stream of customers.

My plan worked. On July 4, as soon as the store opened, we were standing outside in protest. Some customers turned around in support, and others shrugged and walked right past us. We spent the entire day at the store. We were hoping our protest would make a difference, but we had no idea our protest had such reach! As a result of our protest and sacrificing the holiday away from our families and friends, top executives from Walmart's regional office arrived to that Selma store and addressed our demands. I commend those executives for hiring qualified blacks to hold the management positions they so deserve.

Marvin remained faithful in his caregiving until Alan could no longer walk. In 1987, Alan was admitted to New Vaughn hospital, where he passed away with his family and friends at his side. Marvin describes how life with his brothers made him feel:

*"I was very close to both of my brothers. Muscular dystrophy was very painful to their bodies at times. It required a lot of patience to do the simple things that we take for granted, such as eating, drinking and walking. As each of them grew older, their ability to walk became worse. One day they would wake up and not be able to walk anymore. Both of my brothers were mentally strong. As a matter of fact, you would never have known they were afflicted with the disease until you saw them. I didn't go to many places with my oldest brother, but my youngest brother wanted to go places and experience life, like everyone else. I don't recall them having many doctor's visits. I describe MD as a disease that I hate, and I pray that one day they will find a cure. If I were to offer advice to other families dealing with MD, I would encourage them to let their loved ones live as normal a life as they can. Don't go around feeling sorry for them because they are going to have enough to deal with. Just be strong for them. The days of both of my brothers' funerals were the two most depressing days of my life. We all were grieving in our own way. My Dad appeared very strong on the outside, but he lost weight. My Mom's bereavement showed outwardly, yet she also showed strength. Both of my parents are very strong. I always and still to this day wonder why I was not hit with MD. I want*

*to believe that it was meant for me to help my parents with my brothers and make their lives as comfortable as possible."*

Marvin Sr.'s words are quite dear to my heart. Though our family endured the heartache and loss of our oldest son, Frederick Jr., and our youngest son, Alan, few people knew that we lost them due to the dreadful disease of muscular dystrophy. Neither of our sons wanted to be treated differently. They wanted to be loved and cared for, and granting their wish was the best gift we could give them.

My grandsons, Alan Reese and Marvin Reese, Jr., have placed their hearts and souls into March4Muscles, the organization they created to spark awareness and raise money to find a cure for muscular dystrophy. I am extremely proud of the dedication, hard work and sacrifices they have made in the name of their uncles, Fred Jr. and Alan. My sons' memories live within the entire Reese family, and we pray that someday, there will be a cure. Our hearts go out to all parents and families raising a child with the debilitating effects of muscular dystrophy. It's a tough battle to fight, but there is strength in numbers, and we must fight and conquer it together.

‿◦‿

I taught school during the day and spent my evenings traveling to various locations for meetings throughout Selma as needed. There was always a rally to attend, a meeting to head, someone to meet with, or a group who could benefit from being enlightened about the ongoing injustices surrounding Selma. So, Alline made certain that my day began with a hearty breakfast, which would sustain me for hours throughout the day. She treated me like a king, and I treated her like a queen. I enjoyed the special time we spent together, reflecting and chatting about life at the end of our day. Alline has the most beautiful hair I've ever seen. And I always loved its bounce and softness. Often, before bedtime, I would help her unwind from her day by asking her to sit comfortably in a chair or alongside the bed while I alternately parted her hair in small sections and applied Blue Magic or Afro Sheen Conditioner and Hair Dress to her scalp. Alline has always taken great care of her hair, but I secretly feel that I should get at least an ounce of credit for her beautiful tresses. (Don't tell her I said that.) Both items were popular Johnson products, a staple in many black family households. Johnson promoted healthy hair and a soft sheen. If I am not mistaken, you might still find both products in your local stores today. No, this is not a hair commercial, but when you love someone as much as I love Alline, you enjoy doing what others may feel insignificant or mundane in order to please the one you love and place a smile on their face. That's true love.

⟿

It was tantamount that I played an interactive role within the school system. I attended every school activity I possibly could. I would stop in the hallway and get to know my students. I chatted with parents whenever I had the opportunity. I was committed to engaging both the students and parents during the Parent Teacher Association meetings. I was dedicated to being approachable and transparent as each moment presented itself. I treated everyone with respect, and I'm proud to state that the respect I gave was gracefully reciprocated.

I taught at the grade school and high school level, and I later ascended to the position of school principal. Upon assuming my new role, I made every effort to accommodate anyone requiring or requesting my assistance. I was committed to remaining visible to the students, staff and parents. I recall meeting with a first-year teacher who was experiencing anxiety and facing challenges as she acclimated to her new classroom. She spoke of the students taking advantage of her due to this being her first week at Selma High School. I listened thoroughly while she described the events which had been taking place. A few of her students were talking during the lesson and were not following any of her class rules. I was young and mischievous once, so I knew the mindset of the students who were posing a problem. I reflected back to when I was a kid and how I misbehaved in class. Whenever I thought there was an ounce of room to intimidate or frazzle a teacher, I would! I can remember telling my friends, "*Ok, fellas. This is an easy one.* We can run all over this teacher!" But as an adult and now the principal of Selma High School, I made discipline among the entire student body mandatory. I advised this teacher that although it was her first week, I was charging her to take control of her classroom. I relayed the message void of admonishment and filled with encouragement. Teaching was a new venture for her, and my objective was to help her proceed in the right direction. I stressed that students must be made aware that proper decorum is a mandate inside and outside of Selma High School. I would not entertain disrespect or disobedience. End of story.

Maintaining her composure and exercising new-found assertiveness, the new teacher pushed her chair back, stood up and smiled. She shook my hand and thanked me. I allowed 72 hours to pass before checking on her. I walked into the classroom shortly after she called the roll that morning. The students spotted me immediately and stopped what they were doing. All eyes were on me. Without saying a word, I acknowledged the teacher by nodding my head. I glanced at each student and slowly exited the classroom without having to speak a word. She had full control of her classrooms from that day on.

I was present at the parent-teacher meetings, and I stressed that teachers and parents remain active in the educational landscape of our children, for they are the future. It was at those meetings that I and other residents of Selma would convene to discuss the injustices we were facing, where I spoke to eager attendees regarding the various injustices in Selma and had discussions concerning the overall climate of the nation.

# LEARNING, LEADING, TEACHING, PASTORING

"Where there is no vision, there is no hope."
George Washington Carver

I can vividly remember one of my bus trips while I was a college student at Alabama State University. I was riding on the Trailways bus line, headed from Selma to Montgomery, Alabama, returning to school from a weekend visit. I enjoyed exploring places I had never been, and I enjoyed meeting new faces. I frequently rode on bus trips with the college choir whenever we were invited to perform by other colleges or organizations. Sometimes, it seemed we were going nonstop. Yes, we traveled a lot. I seized every opportunity to perform with the choir, and I loved watching and hearing other college choirs perform as well. But on this trip, I thought I'd relax, enjoy my ride and read a book along the way back to school.

The day was bright and sunny, and I planned to ride in style. I was wearing my dark blue suit, my newly shined shoes, my crisp, white shirt and my favorite pinstriped tie. As I proceeded up the steps of the bus and casually walked on, I veered across

81

either side of the aisle as I attempted to locate a place to sit. Midway down the aisle, I spotted an empty seat. But before I could sit down, being the gentleman that I am, I offered the seat to either of the two black women who I immediately noticed were standing. They both shook their heads, *no*, declining my offer. Including the only other black gentleman who was also standing, and the two women who refused to take the empty seat, we were the only four black people on the bus. I refused to stand up after paying for a seat which was in perfectly good shape and was also unoccupied. So, I politely walked over and sat down. The black gentleman who was standing looked over at me, then veered toward the bus driver, and then stared back to me, with a look of sheer shock in his eyes. I could hear the two black ladies gasping in unison. The shorter lady stood still. Her mouth gaped open while she simultaneously used her fingers to grapple the lower part of her neck, atop her collar bone. One would imagine that she had on an invisible strand of pearls. But I was a bit tickled on the inside as I observed her reaching for an object that wasn't there! I heard the sound clearly as the taller, more distinctive woman inhaled a quick gasp and appeared to hold her breath in anticipation of what would happen next. Meanwhile, the bus driver was watching the entire scene through the rear-view mirror as if he could not believe what was unfolding right before his eyes. His stare targeted me from head to toe. I thought, *maybe he's admiring my attire.* Unbothered by it all, I sat down, straightened my tie, slid all the way back and shifted into a more comfortable position in my seat. I felt the eyes of everyone on the entire bus glaring at me. I looked around with a nondescript expression and proceeded to read the book I had retrieved from my travel bag. Although the white people on the bus relented, I knew I had a right to sit in the unoccupied seat, and I held no fear of anyone attempting to stop me. Not another word was spoken, and my bus ride was a pleasant one.

I returned to Selma an educated man, having graduated with a major in secondary education (science/mathematics). I possessed a passion for teaching and wanted to share my college experiences and impart so much of what I had learned to others, especially the young people. Affording me the opportunity to do just that was Dr. C.C. Brown, pastor of the Reformed Presbyterian Church and coordinator of the Presbyterian Schools in Wilcox County. I saw him one day as I was on Jeff Davis Avenue. He was standing in front of the church building. We greeted each other in the true Selma style: with warmth, a smile and a strong handshake. Dr. Brown smiled at me and threw his arms around me as we embraced. He gave me two strong pats over the top of my head and stood back, looked me over and told me how good it was to see me.

"Isn't this a sight for sore eyes? It's Frederick Reese! In the flesh. You must catch me up on your travels. What have you been doing with your life, son! How are you?"

I shared with him with the extensive list of things I had been involved in and how well I had done in college and discussed the civic organizations I was affiliated with.

"Impressive, Frederick. Impressive."

After discussing an array of topics both large and small, interjected with jokes and laughter, the tone of conversation steered directly to business. Dr. Brown informed me that there was a dual vacancy as science teacher and assistant principal at Wilcox. The former principal had recently passed away and he was taking that position, leaving a vacancy for the assistant principal's spot.

"I really like you. You've acquired the education and you definitely possess the qualities and qualifications we're looking for in the person to fill this position, Frederick. Would you consider applying for the vacancies and serving in these roles at Wilcox?"

I just stood there for a moment and smiled.

He asked, "Is that a "yes?"

I looked at him, as I smiled again. I replied with a simple, "Yes."

"That's great, Frederick! I have no doubt that you will make a positive impact at Wilcox! I want you to report to superintendent A.J. Jones' office first thing in the morning. Let the secretary know that you are there to see Mr. Jones. She will be expecting you. Advise Mr. Jones that you would like to apply for both the science teacher and the assistant principal position. Tell him I sent you."

I couldn't believe what I was hearing. I was honored to be recommended for not just one amazing position, but two! I smiled and asked for additional details, and we ended our conversation. This was confirmation reinforced. Education is essential. I didn't have the job or jobs yet, but I knew that I had the credentials and the backing of Dr. Brown. I planned to get a good night's sleep, put on my best suit in the morning and extend the superintendent the pleasure of meeting Frederick D. Reese. And sure enough, that's exactly what I did. And after speaking with Superintendent, A.J. Jones, the next day, I walked out of his office a happy man. I was hired for the job. Or shall I say, both jobs!

The Wilcox County Training School was previously owned and operated by the Presbyterian Board of Education. The school relinquished its operational responsibility to the Wilcox Board of Education. I'm not certain of the reason, but they continued to maintain the operation and upkeep of the Presbyterian Church building, the homes of the principal and assistant principal, the girls' and boys' dormitories, the teachers' dormitories (women's and men's) and the home of the groundskeeper. Oddly enough, the school itself was located on a plantation owned by a white man. Also on the plantation was a "general store." Sharecroppers could purchase items from household goods to household groceries at this special store. Unfortunately, this currency held no value anywhere else. If the sharecroppers desperately needed cash, they could exchange the plantation currency at a much lower face value. Definitely not a fair deal for a sharecropper in need.

My first day as a science teacher and assistant principal was quite rewarding. I enjoyed the best of both worlds. I was afforded the opportunity to impart knowledge and mentor the youth as a teacher. I guided them in their academic studies, and my objective was to extend their learning as far as I could. I made them aware of the importance of education while helping them to apply the fundamentals of science and excel in all that they do. I would not settle for anything below my standards. As assistant principal, I demonstrated my ability to work with the principal and serve as a voice for the teachers. A liaison, if you will. I provided an "open door policy" for the teachers. I wanted them to be aware that I was there for leadership and guidance. I was not there to talk down to them. I was there to provide an element of cohesiveness, not division. It wasn't long before I began noticing inconsistencies and unfair treatment between the black and white teachers at Wilcox. I listened to the teachers who weren't too afraid to speak of the unfair treatment. I began asking questions and gathering facts. Knowledge of the disparate treatment could no longer go unchallenged.

After two years of serving as assistant principal and science teacher, I was elected President of the Wilcox County Teachers Association. I excitedly delved into my responsibilities, as I wanted to play an integral role in eradicating the unfair treatment of teachers.

Shortly after I was elected President of the Teachers Association, I was in attendance at a scheduled meeting with the Wilcox County superintendent and an Education Resource representative. I questioned the intentional delay in the mailing of black teachers' paychecks on the first of each month. You see, black teachers were incurring excessive fees by the bank, as they had to travel to Pineapple, Alabama to retrieve their paychecks in order to receive them more expeditiously. Otherwise, they had to wait long periods of time before the checks arrived via U.S. mail. The white teachers were receiving their paychecks by mail each month like clockwork. And it was disconcerting to learn that the distance from Selma to Pineapple was nearly 50 miles.

By no means was I silent regarding this issue. Meeting

after meeting, I questioned these practices and demanded both an explanation and subsequent action. The majority of the teachers were afraid to voice their complaints because they were apprehensive about losing their jobs, and I definitely would not condemn them for their position. Many teachers sat quietly during the meetings. Others appeared as though they would start to say something, then have a change of heart. I, on the other hand, failed tremendously at holding my peace. It was extremely unsettling for me when I witnessed injustice for anyone. And I could not allow the administration to continue with such a disservice to black teachers. As a leader, I had to stand for what was right and continue to address the problems at hand. I demanded dialogue, as I would not be ignored and I wouldn't stop until something changed. I was not concerned about the resistance I was facing, and I did not mind standing alone. If no one else would stand with me, I was unbothered because I knew I was right and I would continue to fight. And that I did. Each meeting, I relentlessly addressed the pay issues. I made sure that neither my presence nor my voice would go unnoticed.

My undying fight was finally digested and acknowledged by the opposition. Eventually, the battle was won. I imagine the Board knew I wasn't backing down and that they needed to change the process if they wanted me off their backs. They eventually surmised that I was going to keep standing and keep talking. There was no other option as far as I was concerned.

I'm pleased to say that during my tenure as President of the Wilcox Teachers Association, all teachers, both black and white, received their paychecks in a timely manner and around the same time. I knew that fighting for the rights of others, standing up for what I believe in and making sacrifices wherever necessary were the ingredients needed to generate change. I realize that the lack of a voice from those who are being denied rights or whose cries go unheard is a disservice to humankind. Neither the core of my upbringing nor the core of who I am as a man of God will allow me to take a back seat and permit the injustices of anyone within my reach to go unchallenged. I enjoyed my life as an educator. I found so much gratification in imparting knowledge and observing the smiles on my students' faces upon achieving an "A" or accomplishing what some may have viewed as a small feat. And what I realize is that I felt the same amount of joy when I fought for an injustice and the outcome was a tangible one, just as I fought and succeeded in making a significant mark on how paychecks were received.

Also during that time, I had issues with the Teachers Associations and the divisiveness therein. Teachers were a part of a group with the same job description, serving in the same capacity. I agree that there may have been socioeconomic or cultural differences among the teachers, but as a whole, we shared more similarities than differences. I saw no reason for there to be an "all white" or "all black" Teachers Association. It was my desire that we come together and build together. After voicing my opinion to the Board and expressing the benefits of joining forces, and after several instances of pushback, the powers that be and the majority of the teachers reached an agreement to discontinue the "all black" vs. "all white," and I was extremely proud.

I knew I had the drive, the motivation and the will to be the force behind change. Deep down inside, I could visualize my future in continuing to heed my call, taking my God-ordained agenda to a higher level. I wasn't completely certain of the "how" or the "when," but I knew the "why," and I certainly knew that God would lead the way!

⟨⟩

I later became an athletic coach for all campus sports. This, too, was a delight. I enjoyed spending time with the young people and using sports to help build their character. Comparable to the fight for justice, my desire was to play a meaningful role in the lives of others and be of service wherever I could bridge a gap. I wanted to make a difference and generate positive results. Serving in this capacity illustrated a diversified component of my skill set. Assistant principal, science teacher, President of the Wilcox Teachers Association, and now, coach. I was able to touch and help shape the lives of many high school students for nine years. And it was a rewarding experience that I will never forget.

It was during my second year of employment at Wilcox Training School in Millers Ferry, Alabama that I met the love of my life, Miss Alline Toulas Crossing. Alline instantly captured my attention. She was extremely pretty and small in stature. There weren't many women around that looked as good as she did. She had long, black, gorgeous silky hair. She had a smile that would light up the room, and I absolutely loved the way she walked. I admired her from afar. Alline was employed as a Bible and Elementary teacher. She resided in the female Teachers Dormitory on campus. I resided in the male Teachers Dormitory located on campus. I saw Alline frequently in the hallway as we would cross paths heading toward our respective classes or while entering or exiting the building. I always walked with an umbrella. One might say that my umbrella symbolized my trademark or merely part of my image.

Well, one day when I saw Alline, my heart skipped a beat, as it usually did whenever I saw her. But this particular day, she was a bit flirtatious and took it upon herself to snatch my umbrella! She just snatched it right from my hand. That small action enticed and intrigued me even more as I was captured by her charm. We instantly struck a felicitous conversation. Incidentally, I found out she had a boyfriend back home. She didn't brief me on the length of their companionship, nor did I inquire. But after our conversation, I sensed we both knew that that relationship was history. And the more this woman spoke, the more my soul gravitated to hers. Not only was she beautiful, but she was intelligent, she possessed a warm heart and she exhibited such a genuine spirit. I loved the way she carried herself, and her walk epitomized class and grace. After one year of courtship, I knew that I wanted to spend the rest of my life with Alline. We engaged in endless conversations. We discussed our goals, dreams and aspirations. She shared her day-to-day experiences as an educator, and I told her about my plight to end injustice while she intently listened. The love between us sparkled like a rare jewel and blossomed like the most precious rose. And after one year of courtship, I proposed and we decided to marry and become husband and wife. God granted me with a gift that I still cherish to this day.

After nine years in Millers Ferry, I decided to tender my resignation. In 1960, I accepted the position of science and mathematics teacher at the R.B. Hudson High School in my hometown of Selma, Alabama. I was stern with my educational requirements. Under no circumstance would I accept mediocrity, complacency or lack of desire for scholastic achievement. My goal was to educate and motivate students to become successful in life. At the end of the first academic year, I was elected President of the Selma City Teachers Association from 1961-1965. With this appointment, I was in a position where I could reach out to teachers as well as students who were 18 years of age or older to register to vote.

Around 1960, the Student Nonviolent Coordinating Committee (SNCC) was incepted as a response to the call for justice and racial equality. A group of concerned students gathered at Shaw University in Raleigh, North Carolina at a meeting spearheaded by a young woman named Ella Baker. SNCC (also referred to as "SNICK") educated and organized those who were being denied civil and political rights. John Lewis served as chairman. Meanwhile, Martin Luther King was President of the Southern Christian Leadership Conference (SCLC). Both organizations were active and instrumental in growing their respective memberships. However, as time progressed, SNCC members communicated that the SCLC operated with outdated views and didn't appear to be progressing at a viable pace. SNCC members were trained to exercise more confrontational mechanisms, while SCLC members prided themselves on confronting issues from a nonviolent mode of operation.

Bernard Lafayette was an SNCC organizer who arrived in Selma to work with the Dallas County Voters League to register voters. James Forman, also a member of SNCC, organized a rally of 300 citizens to come to the Dallas County Courthouse to register on one out of the two days that allow individuals to attempt to register to vote. October 7, 1963 was referenced as Freedom Day.

In 1962, I was called to pastor Macedonia Baptist Church. I was installed on July 2, 1962. Services were held on the second and fourth Sundays, and in 1963, I was named pastor of Mt. Zion Selfield Baptist Church, where services were held on the first and third Sundays. I enjoyed studying, preaching and teaching the word of God. I maintained a healthy balance between family life, pastoral duties, educational responsibilities and leader of the movement.

As a result of my daily talks with God and the nurturing of a burning feeling inside, I felt compelled to heed a new call and venture in a different direction. I had contemplated running for public office for some time. I had discussed it with Alline, and she remained supportive as always. I realized that my commitment to marching, mentoring and working alongside the SNCC and the SCLC could be more impactful if I held a seat on the Selma City Council. I wasn't tiring of the fight, but I wanted the ability to fight from a different angle and represent the citizens of Selma from a formal ranking. A seat on the council would allow me to be a decision maker and have a true voice in city government. I was one of the first black men to run for City Council in Dallas County since Reconstruction. Although I did not win the seat at that time, I gave Seat 1, Ward 5 a memory to be reckoned with.

I knew that the chances of winning were slim, but I wanted to be an example to the people of Selma, and more than anything, I wanted to set an example for my children. I never took a seat to adversity or rejection. I was defeated, but I was not deterred. I would strive to work harder and focus on my goals, and I knew that someday, I would run again. Upon seeing the imbalance in the white/black ratio of committee members within the Dallas County Democratic Executive Committee, I later led protests and encouraged blacks to run for positions within the committee. While the naysayers felt I was out of my mind and that my fight would be ineffectual, I simply dismissed the negativity and pressed on. I knew that with persistence and the right approach, I could convince blacks to run for various positions. As a result, blacks won, and blacks have filled positions since then. Need I say more?

With persistence comes sacrifice. After speaking to the youth involved with the movement, working alongside the members of SNCC and other local leaders, I took part in yet another march involving the young people of Selma. The youth were excited about their involvement. They expressed a desire to go house to house, pass out flyers and exercise their right to protest and stand up when their parents were afraid to do so. The young people were spreading their wings and getting involved. Many parents were afraid to march, so many students felt compelled to march in their stead, because they were not in jeopardy of losing jobs or homes, as were their parents. That year, in 1964, I was arrested and charged with contributing to the delinquency of minors. Although I felt the charge was exorbitant, I knew that I was making a point and making a stand. And I sat in a cold jail cell as a consequence. I didn't mind the sacrifice. I knew that it was worth it. Youth are quite impressionable, so I had no bending capacity where justice was concerned. As long as I knew deep in my heart that I was doing what was right, I did whatever was needed to get the job done.

It is my belief the sheriff's department felt the need to send a warning signal to the students in an effort to demonstrate what would happen to their parents, given their participation in a march of any kind. However, this only made parents angrier and more inclined to join the movement. Gradually, they did. There was also an increase in the number of participants in the mass meetings.

On numerous occasions, we would rally large numbers of people and walk with them to the courthouse to register to vote. Some were transported by car. We were aware that this type of activity would agitate Sherriff Clark, but we had a mission to fulfill. The constant flow of those being brought to the courthouse drew attention from the news stations. Sherriff Clark would appear with his billy club and posse, and they would swing at everyone within their reach. The cycle continued. Groups would go to the courthouse, only to be denied access and turned back. From there, they would return to the mass meetings at the church, testify and discuss their motivation to follow the same process and do it all over again. Our example sparked others to fearlessly join the fight.

One important note regarding our protests was that we did not condone physical retaliation. We fought back by using our words and strategies. And although tempers flared and it was difficult for some to maintain composure, I advised everyone during our marches that violence was not a part of our platform, and that we were to proceed in decency and in order. Whenever the local news broadcasted encounters with protestors, Sherriff Clark and his posse, the footage repeatedly displayed Clark and his team as the aggressors. Those of us who were protesting always maintained a sense of decorum.

# HOW MANY BUBBLES
# ARE IN A BAR OF SOAP?

" *A*nd thou shalt teach them ordinances and laws, and shalt shew them the way wherein they must walk, and the work that they must do."

Exodus 18:20 (KJV)

I recall one of many failed attempts in registering to vote and being successfully included on the roster of registered voters in Selma. That particular day, I walked into the Dallas County courthouse and approached the registrar at the desk. "Good morning, sir. I'm here to register to vote," I said, arriving in my signature uniform: a nice suit, a neatly pressed shirt and freshly shined shoes. Appearance meant everything to me, and I made certain that I was professionally dressed at all times and that I always conducted business in a professional and respectful manner. The gentleman at the registrar's office clearly demonstrated that he was cut from a different cloth and represented a stark contrast to my interpretation of common courtesy. I wasn't surprised.

Void of an offer to provide me with any paperwork, and neither making eye contact nor properly acknowledging my presence, the gentleman at the desk was committed to the newspaper, which he appeared to be reading silently. I was secretly amused that in his silent reading, he was moving his lips as he perused the contents. I straightened my tie and gently cleared my throat in an attempt to gain his attention. I stood for a few seconds before repeating my prior statement, "Good morning, sir. I'm here to register to vote." Continuing to "lip-read" his newspaper, he paused. Without taking his eyes off the newspaper, he abruptly pointed his finger in the direction of a nearby jar and asked, "How many jelly beans are in that jar?" I stood in silence as I glanced over at the candy-filled jar and then glanced back at Mr. Newspaper. I did not say a word. Using his right index finger and thumb finger, he slowly lowered the handle of his spectacles as his eyes veered over the rim and zoomed directly at me. "I said. How… many… jelly… beans… are in… THAT… jar?" I could see both sternness and amusement on his face as he repeated the question for now the second time. Maintaining an undisturbed expression on my face, suppressing the instantaneous thoughts swirling through my mind, and remaining completely calm, I responded, "I don't know." I looked Mr. Newspaper directly in the eyes as I gently clasped my hands in front of me, and he returned my equable look with a scowl, saying, "Leave this office, nigger." Neither shocked, offended nor taken aback by his retort, I politely turned on my heels. I proudly stepped away from the registrar's desk, and I tread down the courthouse steps. I was somewhat "bent," but I was far from broken. I had become accustomed to this type of response to my attempts to register to vote, as had many others during this time, and for many years prior. And although this was a familiar outcome, it only energized me to work harder. I always hoped for the best, but I was never blindsided by reality.

The registrar's office turned away numbers of black voters on a daily basis. I and others shared our voting experiences during the many mass meetings, which were held at the church and various other meeting places. Once the injunction was in full force, we had difficulty locating a venue where we could meet and make plans due to the thoughts shared by those who feared the repercussions. Whites were literally stalking us and keeping track of our whereabouts. Many places where we had met before and every single church we asked denied our request to hold mass meetings on their premises due to potential backlash. But God! There is always a ram in the bush. We were extremely thankful for Rev. L.L. Anderson for graciously opening his doors and allowing us to host a mass meeting at Tabernacle Baptist, where he served as pastor. The meeting that day was a successful one.

I was the first to arrive at the church. One by one, people began to flow into Tabernacle. I could see the uneasiness on their faces, but there was something about the stride in their walk that displayed fearlessness. I was proud of us all. Somehow, I could feel the spirit of strength and courage move throughout the sanctuary. I was aware that everyone in attendance was making a sacrifice, but joy filled my soul to know that as a whole we were unstoppable. Although the number of mass meeting participants was on the decline, I knew that the majority of those still standing were there for the long haul.

After I and other ministers and leaders welcomed those

who'd arrived, I proceeded with scripture and a prayer, asking God to give us the strength we needed to make it through. I felt a recharge in my faith each time I looked into the eyes of the people. Whenever I spoke, I believe God was wrapping his loving arms around me and allowing my words to charge and recharge many of the people who were within earshot in the sound of my voice. *"We can't give up. And with God's help, we won't give in."* I could see beyond what things appeared to be. I shared my thoughts of how I knew that God would make a way and that He never lets us down. I lifted my hands, closed my eyes and said, *"What a mighty God we serve!"*

Barriers and stumbling blocks were relentless amidst the fight for voting rights in Selma. Each day, we fought some type of battle. Whether we were standing in line at the courthouse, walking along the streets in protest or simply speaking with our neighbors, we were constantly treated as second-class citizens. Whites would throw items at us, call us names and make comments regarding our challenge to register to vote. Some would mock us, bending over as if they were experiencing excruciating pain while being beaten. Being mocked and taunted in Selma was par for the course during that time. I was committed to cure hate with love. I frequently brainstormed, exploring ways to build a virtual bridge to merge us as people, as children of God, and somehow create a united front. I was committed to being a voice for the people. I had to continue to fight, and I had to fight with intensity. As a leader, I had to uphold my faith. I wanted my actions to exemplify my ability to stand for what was right no matter the cost, no matter the consequence and no matter the length of time it might take. After each failed attempt to vote, I could feel a change coming. Somehow, some way, I knew that my current circumstance would not be my story's ending. I knew that I would not allow the oppressors to write my story. With God as the head of everything, He was in charge of my life. He is the author and finisher of my faith. He would write the ending of my story.

"Good morning, sir. I'm here to register to vote." I would stand patiently until I was acknowledged. Some days I would be addressed right away, and other days I stood until I was exhausted. After completing the necessary paperwork, I would wait to be called. I would then answer a set of verbal questions pertaining to the Constitution, the judicial system or one of many irrelevant topics they chose for me to provide responses to THAT day. At times, I felt like telling them how I really felt, but I didn't want to cause a scene or further jeopardize my chances to vote. I encouraged others to do the same. It was my desire to serve as an example, especially to the teachers. The teachers remained our largest number of professionals, and we desperately needed them to continue fighting until we all could vote. I wanted all who had not yet been granted the right to vote to understand that no matter how hard it seemed and no matter how dark things may have appeared to be, day comes after night, and the sun was definitely going to shine again.

Although it was somewhat humiliating many times, I proudly answered the questions that were asked me. Silently praying to God, I asked Him for strength, perseverance and relief. *Lord, please grant us victory over the horizon.*

101

But God! On the appointed date, I walked into the registrar's office and exited as a registered voter! I left the registrar's office a happy man! I reported my victory at the next mass meeting to spread the word and pass the baton of faith. For me, persistence paid off. I never gave up, and I give all the glory and honor to God. He allowed me to fight courageously and remain focused on my ultimate goal. Everyone must remain faithful and never give up.

> *In the past, select blacks who were granted the right to vote could be chosen as a "voucher." A voucher was someone the whites viewed as an upstanding member of the community. If that individual vouched for you, they would recommend you to the registrar's office, and that recommendation could result in a greater chance of becoming a registered voter.

At the next mass meeting, I announced to everyone that I had been granted the right to vote, a right for which they too should fight. I referenced the 1st and 15th Amendments, as I had done so many times before, *"Remember, we have a right to peaceably assemble, and we also have the right to vote. As citizens, we must continue to stand until we are granted the privileges we have a right to possess. We must keep pressing on and encourage others to do the same. We have to fight together and stand together!"* Many in attendance agreed and offered a round of applause. Attendees began to stand up and share their experiences in attempting to register to vote. One lady stood up and trembled in anger as she shared her account. *"The last time I went to the registrar's office, I was asked a stupid question. Do you want to know what that question was?"* In unison, the crowd replied, "Yes." She continued, *"How many bubbles are in a bar of soap? Can you believe that?"* Sadly, no one was surprised. Many had been asked the same question, and others had already heard about the bubbles and the bar of soap question. This type of treatment was wearing down some of the strongest fighters. The consensus was that there was no end in sight. Many were becoming infuriated with the insidious process and lack of respect. Many citizens of Selma were lamenting the constant discrimination and disregard for voting rights. One gentleman exclaimed, "*There has to be some remedy for this! I'm tired of it!*" I agreed with him. People were becoming increasingly discouraged. They were afraid to come out and be a part of the mass meetings, and they were afraid to protest for fear they would be beaten, arrested or killed. Participation was declining, and fear was rising…*something had to be done.*

# THE COURAGEOUS EIGHT

"*P*ut on the whole armor of God, that ye may be
able to stand against the wiles of the devil."

Ephesians 6:11 (KJV)

As a result of the injunction and continued injustices and disenfranchisement flowing throughout Selma, I and several other members of the Dallas County Voters League steering committee decided to create an alliance, organizing a small group to hold a clandestine "meeting of the minds" as a vehicle to discuss issues, concerns and strategies in an effort to advance the voting rights movement. The cycle of individuals being denied the right to vote had been perpetuated for too long. The momentum was weakening among the citizens of Selma, and we had to take a stand.

The first meeting lasted for a few hours as we established our roles. I spearheaded the group. Along with myself, group members included Ulysses Blackmon, Amelia Boynton, Ernest L. Doyle, Marie Foster, James Edward Gildersleeve and Rev. J. D. Hunter. The group often met at private venues, which

105

included our respective homes, to discuss strategies, share information and stage plans of action. There were many citizens of Selma and beyond who looked forward to the day when all people, regardless of race, creed or color, would be granted the right to vote. However, fear overshadowed their desire to break the order, as the risk was too high, and understandably so. Fear of losing jobs or being arrested were common concerns among those of us who wanted to speak out but were afraid to do so. Others were notorious for speaking up, speaking out, marching and protesting. We had unending faith and hope. More than anything, we had courage. Thus, the name Courageous Eight. While we remained professional and nonviolent, some thought we must have been out of our minds to go against the grain. We were fearless and headstrong. We have also been referred to as the "Crazy Eight," but due to the outcome of our efforts, Courageous Eight is the phrase by which we are more commonly recognized. Many people are not aware that I and the members of the Courageous Eight weren't just steering committee members. We shared a mutual respect for one another, and we were friends. Our reputation preceded us in many cases. Once we faced the U.S. Justice Department. They met with us and advised us to put a stop to the mass meetings and marches. They were cognizant of the fact that the Courageous Eight was a force to be reckoned with in Selma. There was no way we would stop. If anything was broken, we set out to fix it, and quitting was never a characteristic of our repertoire. To us, they were speaking without sound. We had heard enough, and it was time we exit. The moment we had enough, we made our move. We made eye contact with one another, turned on our heels, and one by one, we walked out.

Among the extensive list of words which could be used to describe the Courageous Eight, the single, yet most befitting adjective that I choose to apply is "unsung." I was honored to have served as President of this didactic, driven and determined group of individuals. I've neither boasted nor attempted to grandstand about my position, and neither did any of the other members. Each of the members of Courageous Eight was singly and collectively infused with humility and purpose. If the world never knew of these members prior to this moment, I am honored to provide the introductions at this time:

**Ulysses Blackmon** served on the steering committee with the Dallas County Voters League (DCVL). In addition, he was a teacher at a Lutheran school.

**Amelia Boynton**, along with her husband, Sam Boynton, founded the Dallas County Voters League and assisted residents with registering to vote in the 1930s. Amelia Boynton became a registered voter in 1934. She owned an insurance agency and was the first black woman to run for office in the state of Alabama. Amelia played an active role as one of the organizers of

Bloody Sunday, which took place on March 7, 1965. She was a playwright. Amelia is commonly known for being beaten so badly on Bloody Sunday that she lost consciousness and collapsed to the ground. During my term as President of the DCVL, Amelia Boynton was a member of the steering committee. She remained active in fighting against the disenfranchisement of blacks and frequently spoke out against inequality, always reaching out to help others.

 **Ernest L. Doyle** served as Vice President of the Dallas County Voters League. He didn't enter public school until he was 10 years old. Ernest was one of 11 children. He was trained in the field of carpentry and interior/exterior decorating after he returned from serving our country in World War II. He was a member of the DCVL during the 1950s, under the leadership of Sam Boynton, husband of Amelia Boynton. He ran for City Council unsuccessfully in the 1960s. In the 1970s, Doyle was determined to pull himself up be his bootstraps and make a statement. He ran for City Council once again. His opponent, a white man, passed away shortly before the election. After the "powers that be" realized they had no legal right to disqualify Ernest L. Doyle, he won the election and was among the first black men, along with myself, William Kemp, Rev. Lorenzo

Harrison and James Kimber, to be elected to serve on the Selma City Council. Ernest L. Doyle was very outspoken and worked very hard in his position.

**Marie Foster** served as a member of the Dallas County Voters League steering committee. She taught literacy classes in an effort to help citizens pass the literacy tests administered by the registrar's
office. Marie didn't complete high school with the rest of her class, but that "pause" in her life did not deter her drive. Marie later went back to school and successfully completed the requirements necessary to become a dental hygienist. She was beaten as she marched across the Edmund Pettus Bridge during Bloody Sunday, in protest for the right to vote. Marie remained passionate and active in fighting against the disenfranchisement of voting rights. She was known for her resilience and determination. Marie Foster registered to vote eight times before finally being granted the right to vote in 1962.

**James Edward Gildersleeve** served as Treasurer of the Dallas County Voters League. He was a teacher, then served as a principal after he returned from fighting for our country in World War II. James Gildersleeve was born into

a relatively well-to-do family. He was instrumental as a member of the Courageous Eight. He, too, once served as President of the DCVL. On more than a few occasions, he told me that I was crazier than he was. He was a true leader, headstrong yet trustworthy in his deeds. He was determined to do all within his power to contribute to the plight in obtaining voting rights for all.

**Rev. J.D. Hunter** was an advocate for voting rights. He reached out to others, as his mission was to impart wisdom and insight concerning the imbalance of registered voters in Selma. He was geared toward spreading the word to as many as possible within his reach. He was a minister with the love of God embedded in all of his actions. A member of the steering committee for the Dallas County Voters League, he also served as President of the NAACP in Selma. Rev. J.D. Hunter was an insurance agent at one of the few black-owned insurance companies in Selma.

**Rev. Henry Shannon, Jr.** had a passion for helping others. He added value to the Courageous Eight by serving as the voice of reason. Along with spreading the word for voters' rights, he was a supportive member of the steering committee for the Dallas County Voters League. By profession, Rev. Henry Shannon was a barber and a pastor.

✧

It was December of 1964 when the Courageous Eight met at Amelia Boynton's home for one of our scheduled meetings. I and the other seven members arrived within moments of each other and immediately began discussing the most recent protests. The meetings were held at the Boynton home due to the injunction invoked by Judge Hare.

We followed the same format we normally followed during the mass meetings. The only difference was that instead of pews filled with a large number of participants, we were down to just eight members in our meeting. However, we were a powerful eight. We sang a song and I prayed. Following our previously outlined agenda, we then shared the names of those recently arrested, and we discussed the amount of funds needed for bail. The Dallas County Voters League had an allotment of funding for that purpose. J.L Chestnut, attorney for the Dallas County Voters League, did well in handling our legal challenges, posting bail for those arrested and providing legal representation and consultation as needed.

Approximately two months earlier, I had been arrested, along with Martin Luther King, Jr., other leaders and a large number of protestors for "parading without a permit." We had executed a march through the streets of Selma leading right up to the Dallas County Courthouse. We knelt on the sidewalk and openly prayed before proceeding to our destination. This particular march illustrated the force behind large numbers. I remember the weather was a bit chilly. We donned our coats and suits and marched to the courthouse. Shortly thereafter, we were transported to a cold, dark jail cell.

"Well, Mr. President. Here we are again."

"Yes, Doc. Here we are."

"Will you lead us in prayer?"

"Yes."

Each time I was arrested alongside Martin Luther King, Jr., he often asked me to lead us in prayer. I would oblige and we would engage in meaningful conversations thereafter. We would discuss upcoming marches and talk about the progress or lack thereof. We often stood together and reasoned together. There were many times when we determined how to deal with a particular situation. Often, when I prayed, I would allow the Lord to direct my path and provide me the words I needed to say. I asked Him for guidance to do what was right. My words would be the combination of a sermon and a testimony. I always shared what God had done for others and what He had done for me. I asked God to keep watch over all of us. I believed in the power of prayer, because I knew what God had done for me. Whenever I was in jail, I reflected on my wife and children. They were strong. Strength was one of the foundations my family was built upon. The best advice I ever gave my children was to always learn to pray and ask God for guidance because we can't see what He sees. Our charge is to trust Him. I wouldn't change anything about my life. Of all the things I've been through, the Lord was able to see me through and bring me through it. I trust Him because He is able to do all things. The times I was away from my wife and children, I trusted the Lord to keep my family. I looked to the hills whence cometh my help and God said he is always with us.

When Alline was interviewed for this book, her views intertwined with mine. Perhaps that's the reason our relationship blends so well:

"I didn't mind the sacrifices I encountered as a wife and First Lady. I knew what was needed, and I was satisfied. My oldest and youngest son had muscular dystrophy. God took care of us. One day, someone threw something on our porch, a fire bomb. But God kept us. He kept us from all hurt and danger. I knew the fire bomb was thrown as a result of my husband's involvement in the civil rights movement, but I ignored all of the negative talk, and I advised my children to ignore it as well. None of us had fear, and we didn't buy into the negativity or negative talk. We trusted God and knew He would lead us and keep us strong. My advice to my husband was, "Stay out there. God will take care of everything." I was never afraid, and I didn't face any challenges as the wife of a civil rights leader. I was proud of my husband as a civil rights leader. I prayed and went to see Cecil Williamson and Benny Tucker, City Councilmen. I knew my husband needed to be recognized. Thanks to them, Selma has a street named Frederick D. Reese Street."

Depending on the number of individuals who were taken into custody, it wasn't out of the ordinary for a voice to suddenly break the silence with a hymn of strength. I can recall hearing soft humming sounds, which seemed to reflect feelings of dismay. Every song was a cry to God to rescue us and make a path. Unfortunately, cries for help from the Lord were being heard more frequently than ever.

If we were lucky, the guards would allow the singing to continue for a short time. Then, we would hear a not-so-pleasant command to end the song: "We don't wanna hear any more singing!" It felt good to know that while the guards had the power to silence us on the outside, they could never block the fervent prayer we whispered on the inside! Upon being released from our cells, the marchers refueled and recharged. It was time to get back to the business at hand. But the threats looming throughout the city caused fear. Judge Hare meant business, and the injunction was strictly enforced. Martin Luther King, Jr. made it known that if he returned to Selma and participated in future demonstrations, he would only return with a proper invitation.

*At the time, the SCLC did not have a chapter located in Selma, as it had been banned. Some members of SNCC and other locals did not want Martin Luther King, Jr. in Selma because they felt that he was trying to "steal the thunder," take over Selma's movement and make a name for himself.

Sitting around the table at Amelia Boynton's home, we discussed how the injunction had caused the momentum to weaken. Lately, the number of participants had dropped, and overall morale was down considerably. The recent arrests and threats weren't taken lightly by the citizens of Selma. We had made so much progress over time, but the recent decline caused us to take another course of action. I advised my fellow

Courageous Eight members that it would be in our best interest to invite Martin Luther King, Jr. to Selma. He was a great orator, and he had charisma. Martin Luther King, Jr. and the SCLC held an impressive record for raising revenue and helping to boost voting campaigns in other cities, and I felt confident in requesting their assistance in working alongside us in an effort to revitalize and resuscitate our beloved Selma. "As leader of the Courageous Eight, I confirm that by written notification, we will invite Martin Luther King, Jr. and the SCLC to Selma," I in a letter that I also signed. Shortly thereafter, Martin Luther King, Jr., along with members from the Atlanta chapter of the SCLC, made their way to Selma, Alabama.

### *Interesting Fact:

*"I was approximately 10 or 11 years old during the time the Courageous Eight were active in Selma. I can remember when they used to meet on First Avenue, which was right across the street from R.B. High School. The building used to be a grocery store, owned by a white man, Mr. Ham. The store was Ham's Grocery Store.*

*A black girl tried to steal an apple one day, and Mr. Ham caught her and slapped her. The children boycotted the store, and it went out of business. When the store became vacant, the Dallas County Voters League moved into the store. Because I was young, I knew something was going on in the building, but it wasn't as it I was going down to the meetings, so I didn't know what was happening.*

*Sometimes, I would pass by the building, and I could see small bullet holes in the windows. That fascinated me. I don't know where the bullet holes came from, but I noticed it on several occasions, and it was just "different."*

*The ground was falling out from under the building. The sewer line was broken, which washed out all of the dirt, and there was structural damage. The building I'm speaking of is no longer there."*

**George Duke Wilson II, Selma, Alabama**

# SELMA TO MONTGOMERY: THAT BLOODY SUNDAY

"*We* are troubled on every side, yet not distressed; we are perplexed, but not in despair; Persecuted, but not forsaken; cast down, but not destroyed."

2 Corinthians 4:8-9 (KJV)

After the success of the Teachers March, I witnessed a surge in the number of participants joining and rejoining the movement within all age groups and occupations. I was approached by students, doctors, barbers, undertakers and common laborers, all who were proud of the successful journey thus far. They were quite eager to learn how they, too, could make a difference in the fight against injustice and the fight for the right to vote.

The aftereffects of the Teachers March and overall uprising for change radiated to Marion, Alabama, where SCLC worker James Bevel began rallying individuals and ultimately used his voice to garner added support in the right to vote campaign.

Joining the organizational and altruistic efforts of James Bevel was James Orange, a young student activist from Birmingham, Alabama. Together, they led marches and protests for the cause.

117

As a result of protesting and voicing his opposition, James Orange was arrested. C.T. Vivian of the SCLC and about 500 people from surrounding areas supported James Orange by organizing a peaceful protest march from Zion United Methodist Church to the Perry County jail, where James Orange was being held. Word about the march spread rapidly.

On the eve of February 18, 1965, state troopers began to surround the church in full gear. Equipped with their billy clubs, gas canisters and rifles, the troopers stationed themselves as if prepared for war. As the marchers exited Zion United Methodist Church, en route to the Perry County jail, the troopers began firing rounds into the air, shooting out the street lights and beating the marchers. Pandemonium caused many of the marchers to disperse in all directions. A small group of them ran across the street and into Mack's Café. Jimmy Lee Jackson, who was a deacon at his church and a civil rights leader within the community, tried to protect his mother and grandfather after fleeing the church to find refuge at the café. Jimmy Lee Jackson was beaten and shot by James Bonard Fowler, one of the officers firing shots. Jimmie Lee Jackson was unarmed and was only trying to protect his mother. After he was shot, he was transported to the last place he would be seen alive, the Good Samaritan Hospital in Selma. Sadly, Jimmy Lee Jackson's life ended approximately one week later.

The death of Jimmy Lee Jackson was the tragic event which precipitated the idea of a march from Selma to Montgomery. It was initially suggested that his body be taken to the steps of the Capitol in Montgomery, Alabama, so that Governor George

C. Wallace would be forced to view firsthand the result of the brutal forces executed by law enforcement against blacks and minorities. It was one thing to hear about the death of Jimmy Lee Jackson, but what better way to make a statement than to see his remains being carried to the steps of the Capitol? However, once this idea was thoroughly considered, the majority of leaders swayed from the idea of bringing that act to fruition. There were no guarantees that the visual display of Jimmy Lee Jackson's body would alter the hearts or minds of the governor. Perhaps that action would have been counterproductive. The atmosphere was becoming increasingly tense. Injustice was rampant. Jimmy Lee Jackson had been killed, and we had also received word that on February 21, 1965, Malcolm X had been assassinated as well.

James Bevel reached out to me and advised that he wanted to garner my thoughts regarding some upcoming activities he had in mind. Upon meeting with Mr. Bevel, I listened to his thoughts of organizing a march from Selma to Montgomery in protest of Jimmy Lee Jackson's murder, and also against the issues of second-class citizenship treatment within neighborhood housing and the denial of community services for blacks. I immediately told him that I thought it was a great idea. This march was designed to protest multiple concerns and issues that required immediate attention. I knew that the majority of blacks in Selma did not own cars, and leaders were unable to provide cars as a means of transportation to the Capitol. To make this venture possible, we would carefully plan and make the necessary concessions to walk the 50 miles from Selma to Montgomery. We also agreed that this march would be executed in a nonviolent manner. James

Bevel was level-headed and was all about the business at hand. He was expeditious in putting a plan in place, and I respected his thought process. It was confirmed that the march would take place on March 7, 1965. We made every effort to begin spreading the word to residents of Selma and surrounding areas. We were excited about the march.

～

I was pastor of Macedonia Baptist Church in Summerfield, Alabama, during the time of the Selma to Montgomery march. Macedonia was a family -oriented, holy ghost-filled place of worship, and I immensely enjoyed my pastorship there. The church was located about 10 miles north of my hometown of Selma. Services were held on the second and fourth Sunday of each month. Since the march was scheduled on March 2, which fell on a second Sunday, my members were concerned that I would cancel our worship service. *Cancel service? Not a chance.* God had been too good for me to proceed otherwise. He had never canceled on me, so I was not going to cancel on Him! Besides, we all needed to hear a word from the Lord… especially on that Sunday.

I advised the congregation that if the Holy Spirit allowed, I would shorten our order of service so that I could head out for my call of duty. I was in charge of arranging the marchers for the lineup, and I also had to allow for travel time to Brown Chapel, where we were set to converge. In the days leading up to the march, my church members expressed their well wishes. As a whole, I always felt their love, and I appreciated the support whenever I was called to participate in the fight for justice. Several of my Macedonia members committed to participate in the march. Those who were unable to participate offered their support through kind words, prayers, hugs or a sincere nod of approval. I thanked God for such a loving church family, and the thought of them "having my back" meant even more.

Church service began. We had altar call, the welcome, a song, an offering and a few brief announcements. I preached from the depth of my soul, and I could definitely feel the presence of the Lord. Just before the benediction, I expressed some thoughts to my members:

*I ask for your prayers this morning as I drive over to Selma. Today, March 7, 1965, marks the day that a number of us are marching across the Edmund Pettus Bridge. As I stand before you, I believe that marching for the injustice of all people is vital. I cannot stand by and witness large numbers of citizens being turned away at the courthouse and discriminated against, simply due to the color of their skin. I cannot overlook how hard we have been fighting against the sheriff, and for all who are being denied the right to vote based upon racially motivated, biased, impromptu concoctions, which the whites have created and labeled as literacy tests and written exams, as a means of determining whether or not blacks will be granted the right to register to vote. A number of those who have failed these tests are our highly educated; those who hold Bachelor's and Master's Degrees! What a travesty! Every law-abiding citizen has a right to be a participant in the political process and should be treated with fairness and respect. And until every citizen is allowed the opportunity to vote and the opportunity to exercise that right, I will do everything in my power to help bring it to pass. While we are uncertain of the outcome of the march at hand, we know who holds the outcome in His hands. May God continue to bless each and every one of you.*

I asked everyone to close their eyes and raise their hands as we looked to God for the Benediction. Afterward, I whispered a silent prayer, but this time it was for myself. I looked over the congregation, and I smiled. I straightened my tie, brushed off the sleeves of my suit jacket, smoothed my lapel and walked to my car. Immediately after I opened the door and sat behind the wheel, I took a long, deep breath. *What a mighty God we serve.* I looked at the edifice of Macedonia with gratefulness in my heart. I placed the key into the ignition, turned it and headed to Brown Chapel.*

During my drive to Selma, I felt uneasy. I was apprehensive about what lay ahead. I wondered if everything would get off the ground as planned. *Would the march from Selma to Montgomery be successful? Would we face the wrath of Sheriff Clark and his posse again? Would we finally be heard this time? Would this march really make a difference?* My trail of questions were yet to be answered, but I knew that I had to continue trusting and believing in God, because my strength comes from Him; and I knew that He held all power over every circumstance.

Ye are of God, little children, and have overcome
them: because greater is he that is in you, than he that
is in the world. (1 John 4:4)

I arrived at Brown Chapel, parked my car and entered the
church. As marchers continued to fill the sanctuary, I was smiling
on the inside. *My, what a wonderful turnout.* The participants
collectively chimed in with motivational chants and shared
positive words of encouragement. With hopes that God and
the angels in heaven would hear us, we joined hands and sang
heartfelt songs such as, *We Shall Overcome, This Little Light of
Mine* and *I Shall Not Be Moved.*

Blessed is the man who remains steadfast under trial,
for when he has stood the test, he will receive the
crown of life, which God has promised for those who
love him. (James 1:12) ESV

The final planning and execution details of the march were
drafted in conjunction with James Bevel and fellow SCLC
member Hosea Williams of Atlanta. Members of the Southern
Christian Leadership Conference (SCLC) and members of the
Student Nonviolent Coordinating Committee (SNCC) were
both scheduled to participate in the march. However, SNCC
was neither a proponent of Dr. Martin Luther King, Jr., nor was
it a proponent of the SCLC. SCLC members made it clear that
they were not in favor of Dr. Martin Luther King, Jr. coming
to Selma. Moreover, and perhaps more effectively hidden from

the world, the SCLC did not want Dr. Martin Luther King, Jr. to come to Selma on March 7, 1965. Why? Because the SCLC surmised that Dr. Martin Luther King, Jr.'s visit to Selma was too risky. The SCLC viewed King as an asset to the movement. They felt that if he was jailed or hurt, it could adversely affect efforts going forward, and they wanted to shield him as a precaution. Though other leaders were willing to take a chance and make a sacrifice, King chose to comply with the requests of the SCLC. As a result, he did not participate in the march that day, instead remaining in Atlanta.

A little-known fact is that prior to SNCC being officially invited to Selma, it was revealed that SNCC secretly sent someone to "snoop" around Selma, which was an "earmarked location" on their radar, to try to gain notoriety as the next place to spark a movement. Truth is, the foot soldiers, myself and other leaders had already inked our fingerprints and footprints throughout Selma's political landscape long before their "snooping" process was underway. However, after I officially invited SNCC to Selma to assist with groundwork already laid, they accepted. SNCC came in and went to work. They spent numerous hours perusing the streets of Selma, recruiting both adults and especially students and young people to join the movement. They infiltrated Selma and helped to place emphasis on mentoring and educating the masses about voters' rights for all citizens, regardless of race or color. SNCC highlighted the ideals of remaining active and informed within the community. Their teachings promoted the idea of being willing to make personal and life-threatening sacrifices for those individual freedoms that had long been denied. They were present with us at countless meetings held at R.B. Hudson High School, Brown Chapel and various other locations.

The reasoning behind the vast majority of the members of the SNCC having a bad taste in their mouths regarding the SCLC and Dr. Martin Luther King, Jr. was attributable to their belief that he was receiving and accepting accolades and honors that were undeserving and misleadingly highlighted. In addition to their concerns about Dr. Martin Luther King, Jr., I was well aware that SNCC was experiencing organizational and philosophical differences. Some of the members within SNCC felt as though the SCLC was too conservative in terms of both their actions and their reactions regarding the fight for the right to vote. As a Selma leader, President of the Voters League and the person responsible for bringing the SNCC and the SCLC to our town, I served as mediator on many occasions in an effort to bring the two organizations together, but there was no negotiating on this matter. Both organizations embodied the desire, the drive and the determination to aid in the fight for voters' rights. However, they just couldn't seem to agree to disagree. As a result of the escalating tension, members of the SNCC withdrew their support and chose not to march that day.

John Lewis was President of the SNCC at the time of the march. SNCC members had communicated that John Lewis' views were no longer aligned with theirs. They felt that John Lewis had a different frame of mind and a different thought process after he returned from a leadership event that was held outside of the country, and SNCC wanted to maintain their operation via direct action as opposed to operating under a nonviolent premise. However, John Lewis did not allow the way his own organization felt toward him nor the dissension within SNCC to sway his personal opinions and unwavering stance. John Lewis arrived at Brown Chapel and joined us in the march from Selma to Montgomery. And he marched alongside Hosea Williams, front and center, with his backpack in tow.

As we assembled in front of Brown Chapel, word began to spread that the state troopers were awaiting our arrival just over the bridge. Initially, we considered altering our route and directing the marchers down Hwy 14 in order arrive in Montgomery. But after I, Hosea and a few others convened and discussed the situation, we decided that we would neither duck nor dodge from anyone. We would face whomever we needed to face in the process. I knew that it was a sacrifice, but it was a sacrifice worth making. Thus, our original plans would remain. We would march across the Edmund Pettus Bridge and straight onto Hwy 80 until we reached Montgomery. In Hosea's detailed outline of the march, his calculations estimated a full, four to five days of marching before arriving in Montgomery, which was approximately 54 miles away. That was the plan. Selma was a straight shot to Montgomery, and that was exactly what we were set to do.

As the participants of the march gathered around, they listened intently as I explained the logistics of the lineup. "I need everyone to form in groups of two. We do not want anyone to get arrested before crossing the bridge. As many of you are already aware, the ordinance forbids the assembly of three or more on public streets for meetings, protests or marches. We must adhere to the ordinance. So, let us please govern ourselves accordingly."

We were both clever and strategic in forming the lineup. The injunction forbade the gathering of three or more to assemble for the purpose of a march or protest, whether it was during mass meetings or while protesting on the streets of Selma. That's why we marched in twos, with three feet of space between each set of two. I walked back and forth, alongside the marchers, making sure that no one deviated from the mandate. Everyone was cooperative and orderly. After several minutes of orchestrating our departure, everyone was positioned, and the big moment had finally arrived. It was time to begin the march.

Contrasting this to the mood of excitement generated by the marchers upon initially entering the sanctuary of Brown Chapel, I now observed that the encouraging conversations, the positive affirmations and even the upbeat songs we were singing had now morphed into a blanket of silence. Some of the marchers were standing in line and looking straight ahead, not even appearing to blink. From the corner of my eye, I saw a tall, distinctive looking gentleman who appeared nervous as he continuously bit his upper lip, and the young lady beside him, perhaps his daughter, who kept rubbing her hands together and alternating her body weight from one foot to the other.

I was happy to see a diverse group of participants. Included in this group were the educated and the uneducated. The ages ranged from young to old, the stature ranged from short to tall, and the build of the marchers varied from thin to not so thin. I recognized students from R.B. Hudson High School. Glancing at the marchers, I saw quite a few familiar faces. I believe that in some poetic way, the weathered soles on some of the marchers' shoes were reflective of the struggle, the strife, the fear and the pain they had endured most of their lives. And if their shoes could speak, they would recite haikus, ballads, sonnets and limericks, sharing heartbreaking recollections of how a walk on their journey truly feels...

*Dear God, in spite of the darkness, please allow them to grasp the wings of faith, rely on a ray of hope and remain confident that brighter days will come.*

Everyone remained silent... the march began.

*Tap. Tap. Tap.* I can still hear the acoustic from the tapping sound of our shoes as our heels made contact with the hard, cold pavement. *Tap. Tap.* We left Brown Chapel, which is located on Sylvan Street (later named Martin Luther King, Jr. Street), traveling to Alabama Avenue, then west on Alabama Avenue to Broad Street. We marched in silence as we turned the final corner toward the bridge. When we reached the bridge, I studied the makeup of its hint of a pale gray color, steel material, and arch-inspired structure. The arch is supported by studded beams which extend from the pavement to the upper portion of the tiered curvature throughout the architectural design. The arch does not obstruct the overhead view. It is built so that one may look up and over either side, and back and forth, through quadrilateral openings, allowing framed views of the sky. On this day, I was able to look up and imagine a quick glimpse of heaven, trusting that God was looking down upon us. There are two lanes on either side of the highway divider, which lies flush on the center section of the pavement. Displayed on both ends of the bridge are the letters which form the name, Edmund Pettus Bridge. Edmund Pettus was a Confederate brigadier and Grand Dragon of the Ku Klux Klan. *Tap. Tap. Tap.* Edmund was now under our feet. *Tap. Tap.* We continued marching. Still traveling in twos, three feet apart...headed toward the incline of the bridge. *Tap. Tap. Tap.* No words were spoken. Complete silence. *Tap. Tap.*

Upon reaching the apex of the Edmund Pettus Bridge, I looked down. All I could see was a sea of blue. There were countless state troopers in blue uniforms, wearing blue helmets and standing alongside and in front of their blue patrol cars. I had never witnessed the sight of so much blue in my entire life. The troopers were parked parallel on Hwy 80 East across the bridge. I witnessed state troopers holding their billy clubs in one hand, while tapping the other end of the club onto the palm of the opposite hand. Time stood still. Like hungry lions waiting to hunt their prey, the troopers began pacing back and forth, studying our every move. They were positioning and preparing to attack at any given time. We were apprehensive, but not deterred, so we kept marching. We had a mission to fulfill, and I knew we had to keep moving. Troopers were adjusting and applying their gas masks, and in the distance, I could see the sheriff's posse, who were stationed immediately behind the troopers. The posse were on horseback, brandishing their whips. We continued marching.

Major Cloud was the leader of the state troopers. He informed us that he had specific orders from George Wallace, who was then the Governor of the State of Alabama. In no uncertain terms, Major Cloud began to speak into his bullhorn:

"It will be detrimental to your safety to continue this march. And I'm saying that this is an unlawful assembly."

I glanced over at the gentleman marching right next to me. He quickly looked away, but I could see the fear in his eyes. I gave him a reassuring pat on the shoulder, but we never exchanged words. I veered around the crowd, observing those behind and in front of me.

"You have to disperse. You are ordered to disperse."

My lips parted slightly as an inaudible gasp of air was siphoned from the pit of my stomach. I exhaled. I cleared my throat, then I swallowed. As I turned my head, eyes panning in all directions, my body stood motionless, but in deep thought. I was processing the battle ahead of us, the scores of those below us and the magnitude of the opposition's presence. We proceeded to march. *Tap. Tap.* We were getting closer and closer to Major Cloud and the troopers, but we kept marching. *Tap.*

"Go home or go to your church!"

Like the beat of a thousand drums, the pulsation in my ears was synchronized with the rapid beating of my heart. I took a long, deep breath. I exhaled. Time stood still. Again, all I saw was a sea of blue. Hosea and John were now at the bottom of the bridge, just feet away from the troopers.

I sent up a quick prayer: *Lord, please protect us and guide us. In Jesus' name, I pray. Amen.*

The marchers remained quiet. Some appeared to be glazed with trepidation. All were quiet. We kept marching. *Tap. Tap.* But the closer we marched toward the troopers, the more voluminous the jeers and disrespectful name calling from the onlookers became.

*"Get away from here, niggers!"* "Why don't you niggers go home?"

"Kill those niggers!"

We kept moving.

"This march will not continue. Is that clear to you? I've got nothing further to say to you."

We did not comply. *Tap. Tap.* We kept marching. The warnings were disconcerting, but we continued to press on. We marched in spite of the volatile atmosphere, only now, our steps had become more sedate, and the tap of our heels to the pavement less commanding. *Tap.* We kept marching. Slowly, but with determination…

I asked the marchers to kneel. And after what took place next, the only sign of calm was the delicate brush of wind in the atmosphere and the sway of the quiet, dancing waves of the Alabama River flowing below us. Perhaps it was the final calm before the storm.

"ADVANCE!"

Major John Cloud ordered the state troopers to move in on us. And that they did. The troopers began charging into the crowd of marchers, toppling us over like bowling pins. Some who recollect that day have described it as being knocked over like dominos. One by one and sometimes in groups, marchers were being trampled onto the pavement and slammed onto the streets of Selma. The troopers began hitting us with their billy clubs. They executed the same amount of force, no matter who they encountered. They held no regard for the females, the young, or the old. I could hear the screams. Many were crying. The troopers were everywhere.

Suddenly, tear gas was lobbed into the crowd. Simultaneously, the sheriff's posse was ordered to attack. The sight and sounds of the horses approaching us was petrifying. High above the crowd, the posse began beating us. They used their nightsticks to beat our heads, necks, sides and shoulders. Pandemonium broke out! I could not believe this was happening in the United States of America. I could not believe this was happening in our town of Selma! This entire trail of events seemed so surreal.

*"We're gonna teach you niggers a lesson. Ha. Ha. Ha!"* There were more cheers and handclapping from those on the sidelines, who were delighted in watching us being beaten, trampled upon and gassed. The hate became contagious, because the groups who were previously watching in silence had now joined the others in spurting rants of racial vulgarities and obscene hand gestures.

*"Get 'em. Get 'em!"* More handclapping. More cheers. Some ejected ear-piercing whistles, while others screamed cat calls.

These individuals behaved as though they were cheerleaders invited to cheer at a sporting event. The physical and verbal brutality, along with the threats on our lives, was no celebratory matter. This was definitely nothing to cheer about. The horses were neighing and trotting as the posse moved throughout the crowd, striking everyone in sight. Chaos was rampant. As I was rising from the ground after assisting some of the trampled marchers, I was struck on the back of my head and on my shoulder. The pain was excruciating. As I looked around to see who had struck me, I grimaced when I reached around toward the back of my head and attempted to soothe the area of impact by massaging the pain.

Just when I thought this moment couldn't possibly get any worse, the tear gas began to travel toward us. It then infiltrated the area where I and others were positioned. Many complained of a severe burning sensation in their eyes, nose and throat. I felt as though the inside of my mouth had been pierced with millions of sharp needles and I was being forced to ingest them. It was horrible! I tried not to panic. People around me were screaming, coughing and yelling that they couldn't see. They were wiping their eyes, gasping for air and frantically waving their hands in an effort to communicate. Mucus was dripping and running uncontrollably from their nostrils, over their lips and down their chins. Many were wiping their faces with their hands or their clothes and using their scarves, jackets or whatever they could in order to shield the effects of the gas. Shock and fear registered in their eyes. Many began to gag and cough involuntarily. Although I needed to breathe in for oxygen, I was afraid that I would inhale too much tear gas. I couldn't just hold my breath, so I had no choice. *Breathe. Breathe.* I felt like I needed air, even though I was outside, out in the open. *Jesus, please help us!* My nose continued to run and I continued to gasp for air. The effects were stifling. I thought I was dying. Others screamed that they were dying as well. This was an unprecedented experience for all of us. We assumed the worst. I could hear someone vomiting. Marchers were lying in the street. Many attempted to rescue others who were more seriously affected by the gas. Cries could be heard from all directions. A gust of wind whirled as another round of gas was dispersed, causing it to cover more ground, diffusing more burning sensations and discomfort. *Jesus!* Marchers' coats, scarves and hats were blowing and swaying in the wind. I saw blood running down the faces of some of the marchers, an aide-memoir of the severity of the beatings the people of Selma endured that day. I could barely see. I was blinking and coughing as I continued to assist others off the ground. Perhaps due to the adrenaline flowing through my body and the grace of God, I wasn't affected as severely as others. I wanted to help as many as I could. We retreated to a field that was adjacent to the east end of the highway to regain our composure and perhaps get the air that we all so desperately needed.

## "Dear God, please help us, Lord!"

After spending about 30 minutes on the field, praying, comforting one another and mentally preparing ourselves to make our way back to Brown Chapel, we briskly placed one foot in front of the other as we walked toward the direction of the bridge… but only to be met with more violence. Once again, we heard the sounds of the sheriff's horse-riding posse. They had spotted us leaving the field, and they changed their course of direction. Already shaken and bruised, both mentally and physically, we faced yet another round of being accosted by the sheriff's posse. This time, they spat specific threats. "We're going to run you niggers over with our horses. You're nothing to us, you niggers!" The posse repeatedly hit us with their long nightsticks as they spat the most deplorable comments and racial slurs one could imagine. We couldn't believe they were extending the parameters of their vicious and ongoing trail of violence. Tragically, we just couldn't rid ourselves of these hostile, volatile predators.

The horses were trampling through neighborhoods and alongside houses, and I was later informed that a horse was as close as to the front door of Brown Chapel. We weren't expecting the violence to continue after crossing the other side of the bridge, but the posse was relentless. We ran in an attempt to arrive at our respective destinations of choice as fast as we could. Some of the marchers were able to make it all the way home. The doors of homes would swing open, as the residents of Selma extended hospitality and temporary refuge for those trying to escape or for those who required bandages, tourniquets, salves or various items of first aid.

Upon entering Brown Chapel, I was met by many who were injured, frightened, overwhelmed and devastated as a result of the beatings and inhumane treatment they'd endured. My heart ached for them. My heart continued to pound rapidly from the exertion of the violence I'd felt and seen during our attempt to reach Montgomery. While we anticipated the possibilities and results from the march, we had no idea that the ramifications would escalate to this magnitude. Yet, I knew we had to keep going, and I knew we had to keep fighting. Although it was a sacrifice, we had to stand for what we believed in. It seemed as though our backs were up against a wall, but we had to continue. This would not deter us. This would not blindside or shatter us. With God's grace, this had to strengthen us.

"Therefore, my beloved brethren, be ye steadfast, unmovable, always abounding in the work of the Lord, forasmuch as ye know that your labor is not in vain in the Lord." (1 Corinthians 15:58)

Brown Chapel appeared to be a recovery zone for soldiers who had been transferred from the trenches during a war. And sadly, the video reels from March 7, 1965, resemble the onset and aftermath of a one-sided war that unfolded right before our eyes. More than ever, Brown Chapel was living up to its reputation for helping to restore the broken, both physically and spiritually. Brown Chapel holds a special place in my heart. After the injunction was put into force, I called every church in Selma in search of a place to hold mass meetings. Brown Chapel was the only church to say, "Yes." In addition to serving as a place of worship, Brown Chapel was serving as a makeshift hospital, a venue for mass meetings and a greeting station for those coming in from all parts of the U.S. If the walls of that sanctuary could speak, oh, what stories it could tell!

The more seriously injured marchers were transferred to a nearby hospital, including John Lewis, whom we learned had suffered from a fractured skull as a result of being viciously struck with a billy club. We also learned that Amelia Boynton had been beaten so seriously she lay unconscious on the street. Marchers were attempting to assist her. Someone from the crowd cried out to Sheriff Clark, pleading for an ambulance to be brought in for Mrs. Boynton. We were told that the sheriff responded by sneering, rolling his eyes and barely glimpsing at the helpless Amelia Boynton. He sucked his teeth and looked back at the marcher as he nonchalantly replied, "Let the buzzards eat her." Without looking back or saying another word, he simply walked away.

I prayed with and read scriptures to those who had returned to Brown Chapel with me. Many of them were sectioned into groups, exchanging the details of their traumatic experience and horrific encounter with the state troopers and the sheriff's posse. Some were still crying and visibly shaken. I spent time with all of them, and I had lengthy conversations with those who were angry and spoke of returning to their homes to retrieve their weapons to retaliate. I, along with other ministers and marchers, expressed our compassion toward all, making them aware that we understood how they felt. However, we had to take the high road. We rationalized that retaliating would only escalate the violence and tension between the residents of Selma and the oppressors. The ends would neither justify nor outweigh the means. Finally, they agreed.

"Repay no evil for evil. Have regard for good things in the sight of all men. If it is possible, as much as depends on you, live peaceably with all men. Beloved, do not avenge yourselves, but rather give place to wrath; for it is written, "Vengeance is Mine, I will repay," says the Lord." (Romans 12:17-19 NKJV)

In addition to those who participated in the march, people from near and far began pouring into Brown Chapel over the next several hours. Both the local and national news stations were broadcasting live during the beatings on the bridge and in the streets. No one, including the news media, anticipated that a march would culminate in a downward spiral, granting the world with a bird's eye view of such atrocity in Selma. The news coverage spanned from start to finish; there were no edits, no commercial breaks, no cover ups... just raw footage of the nonconfrontational, nonviolent marchers who were subjected to inhumane treatment by state troopers and the sheriff's posse. We had no preconceived notion that mayhem would unfold and shine a spotlight, exposing the radical activities which derived from sheer hate. Scores of those who were eager to pull up their sleeves and get to work offered their support and reached out to the people of Selma. Representatives from multidenominational, multiracial and various socioeconomic backgrounds began to grace the doors of Brown Chapel, extending their hands and hearts in an effort to usher Selma and the nation into a better state.

Later that evening, I can recall a vivid memory as if it were yesterday. The time was around 6:00 pm. As I was praying, meditating and reflecting on the day's events in the sanctuary of Brown Chapel, the phone rang in the pastor's study.

I eased the phone off the hook and answered, "Hello?"

"Mr. President?" It was Dr. Martin Luther King, Jr. Shortly

after Martin and I first met and he was made aware of my position as President of the Dallas County Voters League, President of the Teachers Association, teacher within the school system, and a leader in the fight for voters' rights, he always referenced me as Mr. President. Martin said that he was impressed and could not believe that a teacher in my given capacity was leading a movement. He often told me that he admired my passion and determination in the fight for voters' rights.

"Yes?" I immediately recognized his voice.

"Mr. President, I understand you had a little trouble down there in Selma today." He didn't say another word. Neither did I.

I cleared my throat and paused before speaking, "Doc…" (While he referred to me as "Mr. President, I referred to him as "Doc.") "You know that is an understatement. We had a whole lot of trouble down here in Selma today!"

I knew he was joking. He frequently joked to lighten the thickness of the atmosphere at times.

"Yes, Mr. President, the events of today have been televised everywhere. Everyone is talking about Selma, Alabama and what was witnessed by the nation." He went on to tell me that he was informed of the tremendous beatings which had occurred across the bridge, and he wanted me to know that the SCLC would stand with SNCC and the people of Selma to fight for and secure the right to vote. He had sent out public statements and a number of telegrams urging members of the clergy and all who would support to come to Selma, Alabama and help us fight for the cause.

"Okay, Doc." We spoke several moments longer and then we ended the call.

A few hours had passed, and the darkness of night covered Selma. Though relatively quiet, remaining in the sanctuary of Brown Chapel were some Brown Chapel members, a few marchers and several residents of Selma. I remained at the church to pray for, console and provide assistance in any way I could. There were so many questions regarding why our struggle continued and when we would get relief. Many concerns referenced that the fight was no longer worth the sacrifice. During our discussions, we were interrupted. Pouring into the church were the passengers from a chartered bus which was filled to capacity. A line of unfamiliar faces. Different hues, heights, shapes, sizes, denominations, ethnicities, socioeconomic and multidenominational affiliations were filling the sanctuary. I saw people with straight hair, blonde hair, curly hair and dark hair! You name it, I saw it! They all walked into the sanctuary wearing big smiles and creating a warm atmosphere.

"We saw the news broadcast today, and we are terribly sorry."

"We're here to help the people of Selma."

"We will do what we can to help fight for voters' rights here in Selma and everywhere!"

"Our hearts go out to all of you. You all were treated so badly today."

Our visitors began speaking and offering handshakes to all of us in the sanctuary. We were elated and in awe! *Thank you, Jesus!* Joy filled the sanctuary, eradicating the cloud of gloom that previously loomed over us once we had crossed that bridge earlier today. A few of those who were discouraged and who had been crying in agony before were now crying tears of joy. We were surrounded by complete strangers who were anxious to join us in the fight for justice! We couldn't have been more elated. Upon speaking to the first set of guests, they informed me that they had chartered a plane from New Jersey! I advised the group that New Jersey is a far distance to travel and support total strangers. But the appearance of these guests marked the beginning of a domino effect. Hour after hour, more people stepped onto Selma's soil and into Brown Chapel Church, expressing their desire to help fight for our cause.

The Selma natives graciously welcomed our guests into their homes. Brown Chapel, Green Baptist and First Baptist church also provided temporary accommodations. Hospitality toward the guests was extended with hugs, smiles, good food and relatively cozy sleeping quarters. I felt a sense of rejuvenation. Although I was somewhat drained from the day's events, I knew there was another phase of work on the horizon. I thanked God for our journey thus far. I traveled home and had a good night's sleep. Indeed, indeed. There was more work to be done.

The day after Bloody Sunday, a lawsuit was filed against Governor George Wallace, requesting clearance to freely protest our right to vote and march from Selma to Montgomery with no interference from the state troopers. We wanted to handle our efforts in decency and order, abiding by all rules and refraining from breaking any laws or encountering any type of retaliation or disruption. But our hope was short-lived and temporarily shut down. Federal Judge Frank Johnson immediately denied our request and prohibited future marches and protesting, pending a decision that was to be determined within the next several days.

March 9, 1965, blossomed into a brand-new day. It was a Tuesday, just 48 hours after the atrocities on the Edmund Pettus Bridge, which literally knocked so many to their knees and caused extreme chaos during our first attempt to march to Montgomery. The temperature was cool on the outside, yet I felt warm on the inside due to the number of supporters who had arrived and were still arriving in Selma as a form of support. Dr. Martin Luther King, Jr. had rallied hundreds, if not thousands, of people to Selma. The population of our once small town seemed to nearly double in size due to the unprecedented influx of people since our interrupted journey the first time we set to march. I had slept well the night of Bloody Sunday, and last night's sleep was notably peaceful as well. I had already prayed and left all of my cares in the hands of the Lord.

Although hope and progress were on the horizon, undeniably, there was more work to do and more marching attempts to be made in order to transform the process and help make the lives of others much better. My focus was getting this "do over" march off the ground. Complacency was not a part of my vocabulary, and I made an internal vow to keep the momentum. I continued to plan for the future, and I was confident that if everyone worked hard, prayed harder and continued to fight, eventually we would be destined to welcome progress.

I briefly spoke with Dr. Martin Luther King, Jr. and several other leaders. As always, we prayed, sang hymns and expressed words of encouragement upon leaving Brown Chapel. From the outside, the dynamics of the march appeared as though someone had pressed the "replay" button from just 48 hours prior. But this time, the number of marchers had swelled tremendously. Yet again, it was time to march. We left Brown Chapel and made our way to the Edmund Pettus Bridge. I had no idea that we were unveiling activities that would later be written into the books of history.

From atop the bridge, we again witnessed the large presence of troopers and the infamous sheriff's posse. Dr. Martin Luther King, Jr. had decided to execute a "symbolic" march in order to make a "statement." His plan was to allow the protestors of this march to display will, determination, solidarity and a rally of support, in spite of the court order, by going through the motions of marching by "definition." Dr. King indicated that he was neither disrespecting the judge nor the order, but we had to demonstrate the act of marching across the bridge. It was mandatory that we moved forward. To this day, many people were unaware of the reasoning behind those actions. Some protestors were visibly upset, and others wore confused expressions on their faces, as they could not grasp the rationalization behind the volte-face. But the majority of moved along in silence and followed the lead across the Edmund Pettus Bridge once again. The reasoning behind the "symbolic march" produced inquiries from every direction. The troopers, the bystanders and the marchers appeared perplexed. Quietly kept from many during that time, President Lyndon B. Johnson had advised Dr. King to make sure that everyone was compliant with the order, ceasing all marching until the order was lifted. By ceasing to march and following the orders, it would allow adequate time for the legal order to take its course, and it would also lend the time needed to coordinate police protection for all protestors during the pending march. So, there was a legal process and a lot of red tape that needed to be cut, but Dr. King knew that many people had traveled long distances to arrive in Selma after his call to the nation. To have so many arrive under those pretenses, and to then be made aware that the march would not take place, whether due to a court order or otherwise, those reasons would not have fared well with the masses. So there had to be a march in some form, if nothing more but to placate the protestors who had traveled great distances in support of Selma. King's plan entailed marching across the bridge, kneeling to pray and then turning around and marching back to Brown Chapel Church. And that is exactly what we did. That day has become known as Turnaround Tuesday.

After we returned to our respective places of choice and awaited the decision of the Attorney General, our hope was that we would be granted clearance to freely march from Selma to our State Capitol in the near future, with full protection from the governing bodies.

Hours later, we learned that three white ministers, Rev. Clark Olsen, Rev. James Reeb and Rev. Orloff Miller, who traveled into Selma to support the march, had decided to dine at Walker's Café, a black-owned diner in Selma. As they were leaving for the evening, they were approached by a small group of white men, allegedly members of the KKK, who referred to the ministers as "niggers" and began taunting them. One of the accosters forcefully struck Rev. James Reeb in the head with a club of some type, and Rev. Reeb immediately fell to the ground. The ministers reported that they witnessed Rev. Reeb in excruciating pain and watched in horror as he held the hand of one of the ministers until he lost consciousness. A nearby black hospital was unable to treat him due to the lack of resources, and a white hospital refused to treat him after they received word that Rev. Reeb was a "nigger lover" and was marching in support of blacks. As his condition steadily declined from the blow to his head and the ensuing lack of immediate medical care, Rev. Reeb was finally transported to a hospital in Birmingham, Alabama. Tragically, he succumbed to his injuries and passed away about two days later.

The death of Rev. James Reeb resulted in an outcry for justice and an even greater outpouring of demonstrations. Many protestors began lining up near Brown Chapel to display their opposition to the continuous violence and disregard for the rights of others. Wilson Baker was Selma's Public Safety Director at the time. He demanded that the protestors leave the area. But the number of protestors was a bit cumbersome for Baker and the Public Safety department. Baker was furious. Not only were the blacks protesting, but there was a mixture of blacks and whites due to the large number of individuals who remained in Selma after the attempt to march from Selma to Montgomery. Baker and his officers began to set up ropes and wooden barricades, also referred to as "wooden horses," on Sylvan Street, which was near Brown Chapel Church. Protestors were leaning up against the ropes, chanting about the injustices ensconcing Selma and holding hands as they sang hymns and songs of praise. The event of blocking Sylvan Street with ropes and barricades is famously referenced in Selma as "The Berlin Wall." Wilson

Baker instructed the officers to be stationed at the barricades 24 hours a day. The streets of Selma were quite busy, to say the least. The scene resembled a standoff. The officers wouldn't budge, but neither would the protestors of Selma, who composed a song while on the streets and began to sing in unison:

We've got a rope that's a Berlin Wall. A Berlin Wall. A Berlin Wall.

We've got a rope that's a Berlin Wall. In Selma, Alabama.

We're gonna stand here 'til it fall. 'Til it fall. 'Til it fall.

We're gonna stand here 'til it fall. In Selma, Alabama.

Hate is the thing that built that wall. Built that wall. Built that wall.

Hate is the thing that built that wall. In Selma, Alabama.

Love is the thing that'll make it fall. Make it fall. Make it fall.

Love is the thing that'll make it fall. In Selma, Alabama.

If the people of Selma didn't demonstrate anything else to the world, the hearts of the people of Selma demonstrated resilience, hope, faith and love. Though many were often beaten, scorned and mistreated, somehow, as a whole we embraced the precept of trying to do what was right. We managed to withstand the adversity we were facing and attempted to stand our ground at all costs, in spite of numerous failed attempts. Through it all, we remained determined, and for the most part, we remained headstrong. What a sacrifice.

The waves of the Alabama River appeared to dance a bit faster. Perhaps it was the sign of a shift. Little did we know a major change was about to take place. About a week or so later, we welcomed the announcement that brought music to the ears of many. Thank God. Thank God. On March 15, 1965, President Lyndon B. Johnson addressed Congress and presented at the platform with a bipartisan speech at a congressional session. I must share the contents of the speech, though lengthy, because it is paramount in framing the picture of how the efforts of the unsung heroes, the foot soldiers, the efforts leading from the Teachers March, the death of Jimmy Lee Jackson, the trail from Bloody Sunday and Selma's sacrifice as a whole contributes to the importance and the significance of the President's speech. Our blood, sweat and tears were the seeds that were planted deep in Selma's soil. And finally, we could begin to see a small bloom beginning to rise from the ground. We were aware that it wasn't a full garden, but we felt like proud farmers who could begin to look across the field, observe the progress of our crops and exhale just a bit, knowing that our hard work was finally producing results:

"At times, history and fate meet at a single time in a single place to shape a turning point in man's unending search for freedom. So, it was at Lexington and Concord. So, it was a century ago at Appomattox. So, it was last week in Selma, Alabama. There, long suffering men and women peacefully protested the denial of their rights as Americans. Many of them were brutally assaulted. One good man, a man of God, was killed. There is no cause for pride in what has happened in Selma. There is no cause for self-satisfaction in the long denial of equal rights of millions of Americans. But there is cause for hope and for faith in our Democracy in what is happening here tonight. For the cries of pain and the hymns and protests of oppressed people have summoned into convocation all the majesty of this great government, the government of the greatest nation on earth. Our mission is at once the oldest and the most basic of this country, to right wrong, to do justice, to serve man. In our time we have come to live with the moments of great crises. Our lives have been marked with debate about great issues, issues of war and peace, issues of prosperity and depression.

But rarely in any time does an issue lay bare the secret heart of America itself. Rarely are we met with a challenge, not to our growth or abundance, or our welfare or our security, but rather to the values and the purposes and the meaning of our beloved nation. The issue of equal rights for American Negroes is such an issue. And should we defeat every enemy, and should we double our wealth and conquer the stars, and still be unequal to this issue, then we will have failed as a people and as a nation. For, with a country as with a person, "What is a man profited if he shall gain the whole world, and lose his own soul?" There is no Negro problem. There is no Southern problem. There is no Northern problem. There is only an American problem. And we are met here tonight as Americans, not as Democrats or Republicans; we're met here as Americans to solve that problem. This was the first nation in the history of the world to be founded with a purpose.

The great phrases of that purpose still sound in every American heart, North and South: "All men are created equal." "Government by consent of the governed." "Give me liberty or give me death." And those are not just clever words, and those are not just empty theories. In their name Americans have fought and died for two centuries and tonight around the world they stand there as guardians of our liberty risking their lives. Those words are promised to every citizen that he shall share in the dignity of man. This dignity cannot be found in a man's possessions. It cannot be found in his power or in his position. It really rests on his right to be treated as a man equal in opportunity to all others. It says that he shall share in freedom. He shall choose his leaders, educate his children, to provide for his family according to his ability and his merits as a human being.

To apply any other test, to deny a man his hopes because of his color or race or his religion or the place of his birth is not only to do injustice, it is to deny Americans and to dishonor the dead who gave their lives for American freedom. Our fathers believed that if this noble view of the rights of man *was to flourish it must be rooted in democracy. This most basic right of all was the right to choose your own leaders. The history of this country in large measure is the history of expansion of the right to all of our people.*

*Many of the issues of civil rights are very complex and most difficult. But about this there can and should be no argument: every American citizen must have an equal right to vote. There is no reason which can excuse the denial of that right. There is no duty which weighs more heavily on us than the duty we have to ensure that right. Yet the harsh fact is that in many places in this country men and women are kept from voting simply because they are Negroes.*

*Every device of which human ingenuity is capable, has been used to deny this right. The Negro citizen may go to register only to be told that the day is wrong, or the hour is late, or the official in charge is absent. And if he persists and, if he manages to present himself to the registrar, he may be disqualified because he did not spell out his middle name, or because he abbreviated a word on the application. And if he manages to fill out an application, he is given a test. The registrar is the sole judge of whether he passes this test. He may be asked to recite the entire Constitution, or explain the most complex provisions of state law. And even a college degree cannot be used to prove that he can read and write. For the fact is that the only way to pass these barriers is to show a white skin. Experience has clearly shown that the existing process of law cannot overcome systematic and ingenious discrimination. No law that we now have on the books, and*

*I have helped to put three of them there, can insure the right to vote when local officials are determined to deny it. In such a case, our duty must be clear to all of us. The Constitution says that no person shall be kept from voting because of his race or his color. We have all sworn an oath before God to support and to defend that Constitution. We must now act in obedience to that oath. Wednesday, I will send to Congress a law designed to eliminate illegal barriers to the right to vote. The broad principles of that bill will be in the hands of the Democratic and Republican leaders tomorrow. After they have reviewed it, it will come here formally as a bill. I am grateful for this opportunity to come here tonight at the invitation of the leadership to reason with my friends, to give them my views and to visit with my former colleagues. I have had prepared a more comprehensive analysis of the legislation which I had intended to transmit to the clerk tomorrow, but which I will submit to the clerks tonight. But I want to really discuss the main proposals of this legislation. This bill will strike down restrictions to voting in all elections, federal, state and local, which have been used to deny Negroes the right to vote. This bill will establish a simple, uniform standard which cannot be used, however ingenious the effort, to flout our Constitution. It will provide for citizens to be registered by officials of the United States Government, if the state officials refuse to register them. It will eliminate tedious, unnecessary lawsuits which delay the right to vote. Finally, this legislation will insure that properly registered individuals are not prohibited from voting. I will welcome the suggestions*

151

*from all the members of Congress. I have no doubt that I will get some. On ways and means to strengthen this law and to make it effective.*

*But experience has plainly shown that this is the only path to carry out the command of the Constitution. To those who seek to avoid action by their national government in their home communities, who want to and who seek to maintain purely local control over elections, the answer is simple: open your polling places to all your people. Allow men and women to register and vote whatever the color of their skin. Extend the rights of citizenship to every citizen of this land. There is no Constitutional issue here. The command of the Constitution is plain. There is no moral issue. It is wrong. Deadly wrong, to deny any of your fellow Americans the right to vote in this country.*

*There is no issue of state's rights or national rights. There is only the struggle for human rights. I have not the slightest doubt what will be your answer. But the last time a President sent a civil rights bill to the Congress it contained a provision to protect voting rights in Federal elections. That civil rights bill was passed after eight long months of debate. And when that bill came to my desk from the Congress for signature, the heart of the voting provision had been eliminated. This time, on this issue, there must be no delay, or no hesitation, or no compromise with our purpose. We cannot, we must not, refuse to protect the right of every American to vote in every election that he may desire to participate in.*

*And we ought not, and we cannot, and we must not*

*wait another eight months before we get a bill. We have
already waited 100 years and more and the time for waiting
is gone. So I ask you to join me in working long hours and
nights and weekends, if necessary, to pass this bill. And I
don't make that request lightly, for, from the window where
I sit, with the problems of our country, I recognize that from
outside this chamber is the outraged conscience of a nation,
the grave concern of many nations and the harsh judgment
of history on our acts. But even if we pass this bill the battle
will not be over. What happened in Selma is part of a far
larger movement which reaches into every section and state
of America.*

*It is the effort of American Negroes to secure for
themselves the full blessings of American life. Their cause
must be our cause too. Because it's not just Negroes, but
really, it's all of us, who must overcome the crippling legacy
of bigotry and injustice. And we shall overcome."* **(Lyndon
B. Johnson Presidential Library)**

When word surfaced regarding the contents of President
Lyndon B. Johnson's speech and his specific reference to Selma,
Alabama, a sense of exhale and joy embraced and comforted the
people of Selma. The President's uttered words from the song
we frequently used to calm our crying souls took on a stronger
meaning at that moment. There was a rebirth to the words, "We
shall overcome." President Johnson's closing sentiment meant so
much to the citizens of Selma. The speech resonated throughout
the land and served as a stepping stone for progress. The address

to Congress represented the overdue recognition after years of protests, fights for injustice and sacrifices made by the Foot Soldiers, known and unknown. Our fixity of purpose and intestinal fortitude earned prominence from a highly respected platform. I experienced an exuberant flow of emotions upon hearing President Johnson publicly address his support for a voting rights bill! I knew our labor had not been in vain. On March 18, 1965, Judge Johnson provided the clearance we were praying for. We were finally granted the right to march from Selma to Montgomery. Governor George Wallace attempted to dampen that victory by refusing to provide protection for the marchers. But God! When President Johnson received this news, he exercised his presidential authority by federalizing the Alabama National Guard and provided the protection we needed in order to march to our Capitol! I was elated.

"Giving thanks always for all things unto God and the Father in the name of our Lord Jesus Christ." (Ephesians 5:20 KJV)

March 21, 1965, marked the day in which the Selma to Montgomery march was officially underway. It was estimated that upwards of 3,000 marchers arrived at Brown Chapel Church that day, but the order limited us to approximately 300 marchers for safety and logistical reasons. As in the previous attempt days prior, there were marchers present, and there were troopers present. The distinguishing factor this time was that many of the same troopers who had beaten, spat upon, trampled and gassed us were now ordered to protect us. I looked above my head and observed the circular motion of the propellers, and I listened to the humming sounds generated by the motor as the helicopters hovered above us. I likened my observation of the helicopter to our struggles past and present and the ongoing sacrifice of the town. I felt that Selma was rising above the obstacles we had fought so hard to conquer, and we were now viewing those obstacles from a different perspective.

"Rev. Reese, we're ready for you on the front line."

As I took my place, I looked over at Rev. Martin Luther King, Jr., then I looked among the growing crowd as I smiled from within and inhaled the crisp, Selma air. I glanced at the large number of gentlemen in uniform who were there to protect us. It was a stark contrast to prior marches, because this time, the sea of blue was representative of a symbol of calm. I thought to myself, *it's amazing how God can turn things around.*

There was an array of emotions that day. Many people expressed feelings of triumph and victory, and there were some who remained reticent to speak or who were reserved toward outward celebration because of their fear that this change of events was too good to be true. I can still visualize the start of the march, and I recall several gentlemen carrying a casket, which symbolized the end of Sheriff Jim Clark's resistance to the fight for injustice and his overall "Never" stance for equality. The sign on the casket read, "Sheriff Clark is dead."

I was proudly serving as pastor of both Macedonia Baptist Church and Mt. Zion Selfield Baptist Church. The day of March 21, 1965, is monumental for me, because I was set to participate in what would later be referenced as the historical march from Selma to Montgomery, and I had also been asked to accept the invitation to be chosen as the new pastor of Ebenezer Baptist Church in Selma. Ebenezer's pastor had recently passed, and I was selected by the congregation to fill the vacancy. I cannot describe the joy I felt on that day.

After prayer, songs of praise and well wishes, the march began. From the front line, I stood arm in arm marching among a sea of proud people of many creeds and colors. We proudly placed one foot in front of the other as we proceeded toward Hwy 80.

"Are you ready, Mr. President?"

"I certainly am, Doc."

I walked the first leg of the march, which was about seven or eight miles. I then had to journey back home for a scheduled meeting with the deacons from both Macedonia Baptist Church and Mt. Zion Selfield Baptist Church. My purpose was to personally advise them of my decision to accept the call to Ebenezer Baptist Church and express how blessed I felt to have served both congregations. I wanted to deliver the news personally and address any concerns they may have had regarding the transition. There was mutual respect among us, and I cherished our rapport. I strove to keep it that way.

I met with the deacons and then rejoined the march as soon as time would allow. The march to Montgomery took five days. When we arrived at the grounds of Saint Jude, which was a multipurpose venue, we were entertained by an array of performers, and we experienced a night to remember. Organized by Harry Belafonte, celebrities came out in large numbers to provide entertainment and demonstrate their support for the Selma to Montgomery march. I can't recall everyone individually, but some of the celebrities included Mahalia Jackson, Sammy Davis, Jr., Shelley Winters, Nipsey Russell, Peter, Paul and Mary, Billy Eckstein, Nina Simone, Johnny Mathis, Lena Horne and Dick Gregory.

The march as a whole was successful. After leaving Brown Chapel, the marchers officially stopped three or four times to rest and receive food for continued strength and refreshment. When we reached the Capitol grounds, I was amazed at how many had joined the original marchers, which resulted in an expansion to more than 50,000 people once we reached our destination. So many people joined the march in order to be a part of this unprecedented, historic event. I sat on the platform and looked out over that sea of humanity as Dr. King made his speech. I thought about all the difficulties that we had encountered, and how we had received some beatings and the denial of the right to march down Hwy 80. I began to thank God for all that He had done for us, for He had brought us safe from Selma, all the way to where we currently stood, in Montgomery, Alabama, the place for which we had fought so hard to make a statement. I thought about all the many people who had sacrificed so much, including their personal time, wealth and fame, in order to receive the benefits of marching from Selma to Montgomery. And to have the privilege of being able to receive the blessings of the Lord for all that He had done for us, it was a feeling I had never experienced before. There were thousands gathered around the platform to hear Dr. King speak. They listened intently. At the end of that speech, we left the march and journeyed back to our respective home. I continued to reflect, and I wondered what else God had in store.

Our efforts, along with Selma's sacrifice, is what prompted the passage and signing of the Voting Rights Act of 1965 (officially signed into law on August 6, 1965). Eradicated are those dreaded days of being forced to jump hoops, take demeaning and degrading literacy tests, suffer public and private humiliation, and lose our homes, jobs and sense of esteem by being asked how many marbles are in a jar or how many bubbles are in a bar of soap! All for attempting to participate in an activity which was rightfully ours all along.

What a joy to receive an extension from Congress that solidified and secured the right to vote for the masses of people who had been long denied. The Voting Rights Act of 1965 also opened the doors for blacks who held the desire to serve as leaders and elected officials and enter the arena of politics. In turn, blacks were finally granted the opportunity to fearlessly take a stand, to have a voice and to possibly secure a position in the political process, making differences and strides both locally and globally.

---

*Note: Although the National Guard was present and set to protect us along the Selma to Montgomery march, word later spread that many of the weapons carried by the guards did not contain ammunition. We can neither confirm nor deny the validity of this statement, but given the history of the oppressors of Selma and given the climate of the hate during the movement, I can only thank God for his grace and mercy...for keeping and covering us, and for allowing no hurt or harm to come our way. To God be the glory!

After the march from Selma to Montgomery came to a close, there seemed to be a "hush" looming over the city. If one walked through the streets, peered through their windows or sat on their front porch, there were no signs of any protesters. Every now and then, a car would slowly cruise along the dilapidated pavement. The driver would either wave or nod his head to acknowledge those visible throughout the neighborhoods of Selma. Hushed were the hustling and bustling sounds of a crowd. Silenced were the songs and hymns of both outcry and melody. The trail of visitors who had nestled into temporary living quarters with Selma residents were now remnants from recent memories. The visitors who were recently seen eating meals, chatting with the locals and patronizing Selma businesses seemed to have vanished into thin air. All of the "big names" and those holding titles of distinction who came to help Selma in the fight had returned to their respective homes and families. Selma's metamorphosis did not leave an ounce of residue from any of those individuals having been there. The pomp and circumstance had fallen into a realm of nonexistence. Everything seemed to layer back to normalcy. Selma was quiet.

Many of the young people felt let down. They lamented in disappointment. Up until then, the young people had spent a generous amount of time planning, strategizing and staging their own protests. They'd expressed how they had absorbed a sense of pride in their contribution to the fight for justice.

During the height of the protests, students would report to school as usual, but they had devised a plan of action. They would get up and go to school as they normally would. They would go to their homeroom class and remain for roll call. Once the teacher called their names, they would answer, "Present," "I'm here," or they would stand up or simply raise their hand. But, after doing so, they excitedly exited the classroom. It is my understanding that one teacher advised the students that he would turn his back after the roll was called, and he hoped he would not see a single student left in his classroom when he turned back around! His wish became reality. He was the only one left in the classroom. It warmed his heart.

This demonstration of solidarity from the young people made the teachers feel proud, and the students felt empowered because they could stand up for what they were fighting for without consequences. The adults couldn't freely protest due to potentially losing their jobs or facing other negative repercussions, so the students enjoyed their contribution to the movement. While they made a statement via their protests, they knew they were fighting for their parents and other adults who couldn't freely express themselves as the students could. They felt empowered.

But there were some of us whose thirst was not quenched, nor were we satisfied with the temporary clearing of smoke after the march. Surely, there was more work to be done. It was okay to "settle" down for a moment, but the idea of "settling down" was never an option.

Rev. Goldthwaite "Goldy" Sherrill was a white, Episcopal pastor in Ipswich, Massachusetts. He traveled to Selma and participated in the Selma to Montgomery march. During the march, he spoke with several local leaders about ideas he had circling in his mind. He was aware of the fight for the right to vote in Selma and could see a mirrored image in Massachusetts. Shortly after he returned home, he reached out to Selma. Rev. Sherrill expressed that he was a proponent of integration and voting rights for all, and that he held the desire to make strides in bridging the gap of injustice and inequality in every way he could. Rev. Sherrill worked with Rev. George Galloway, myself, Andrew Young and other members of the SCLC in talks for a special project. His vision was to allow the young people in the north and the south to join forces and continue the momentum via a new thoroughfare. Rev. Galloway, Ms. Lilly (Rev. Galloway's assistant), myself, and Mrs. Bevel carefully selected 36 students to board a bus for a trip to Ipswich, Massachusetts! The students from Selma were afforded the opportunity to travel to a place they had never been, visit sights they had never seen and assist those far from Selma with their fight for the right to vote. The trip was enlightening and well deserved for those students selected. They came back with stories to last a lifetime as they spoke of their experience. Many thanks to Rev. Galloway, Rev. Sherrill and all others involved for an experience of a lifetime for many of the students.

Good deeds seemed to have been working in our favor. In addition to sending our youth to Ipswich, Massachusetts, I was presented with $7,000 from Rev. Gilbert Caldwell, pastor of Union Methodist Church in South End, Boston. Once again, Selma's sacrifice was being revealed to many. People from all around began to reach out and provide the funding needed to continue our fight to make certain every citizen would be granted the right to register to vote. The money I received was generated from the proceeds raised in Boston, a war cry to aid Selma as a result of Rev. James Reeb's death on March 11, 1965.

⟿

Following Bloody Sunday and the march from Selma to Montgomery, there were those of us who were inoculated from complacency. I and the members of the Courageous Eight were well aware that the Selma to Montgomery march was merely a stepping stone as far as progress was concerned. While the march resulted in an enormous sense of awareness and pride and placed the small of town of Selma squarely on the minds of many around the world, we had to keep the momentum. If this moment in time was a sentence, it would closely resemble a comma…but never a period. So, I rolled up my sleeves, and so did Marie Foster, Ernest L. Doyle and a few others. We continued to meet and discuss plans of action. I sat in on several meetings with the mayor of Selma, Jim Smitherman.

"We must make a concerted effort to improve the black neighborhoods, Mayor Smitherman" I told the mayor. I stressed that many Selma residents were subjected to poor living conditions, and the roads leading to their homes and surrounding locations were in desperate need of repaving, revamping and revitalization. "Many of the roads in our town are deplorable. We don't have nice parks in which our children can swing on swings, play in the sand or simply engage in the gratifying playtime in which kids are drawn to participate." Smitherman listened intently while I spoke. He knew that since the march, there was no stopping for many of us. And I knew my fight had only been recharged. I spoke with members of the county government to make a plea for our youth to have summer job opportunities. As evidenced by the manner in which the young people of Selma rallied and organized as a result of their connection and mentorship with SNCC, they demonstrated maturity and executed great strides in making a difference within the community. It would be in the best interest of the students and the city of Selma to create jobs in order to keep our youth occupied and involved, connecting them with opportunities to learn the concepts of employment and make a contribution to society. This would instill values and goals within them and plant the seeds which would last a lifetime. The summer program was successful.

I arranged a meeting and brought to the attention of the Retail Merchants Association that Selma had a disparaging number or outright lack of black clerks in local clothing stores, grocery stores, and pharmacies and banks. I expressed that while whites were the majority employed, blacks were frequenting these establishments and spending our dollars there. It was high time to open the doors of opportunity to blacks who met or sometimes exceeded the qualifications of whites who were monopolizing positions and denying blacks an equal opportunity. My purpose was not to discredit or exclude whites. My purpose was to provide the same opportunities for qualified blacks. I can proudly state that shortly thereafter, one could walk into many of the stores they frequented and would be welcomed by both black and white clerks and cashiers, a sight which had not been frequently seen before. It was a sight that warmed the hearts of Selma.

The fight continued, as I convinced residents of Selma that we needed to apply the same pressure to the banking industry. Upon walking into any bank in Selma, every employee was white. Opportunities for blacks to work in the banking industry were null, and changes had to be made. A meeting was arranged, and conversations took place. The presidents of several banks agreed and shortly thereafter met our demands to hire blacks in the industry. The initiatives set into place were changing the landscape of Selma. I felt that we should tackle every concern one by one.

I led not just one, but several demonstrations against the local newspaper to protest the ways in which blacks were depicted and discriminated against. Selma's population was majority black, and more often than not, blacks were treated as substandard, second-class citizens. This was the reason why the marches, namely Selma to Montgomery, by no means represented an end to the disenfranchisement of voting rights or the existence of racial inequality. There were many blacks in Selma who read the newspaper for knowledge, insight, information and relaxation. However, many of us had endured the sight of the "Nigger Page" and "Colored News" section long enough. In addition, the titles of "Miss" or "Mrs." were never applied when referencing black women within the articles. They were always addressed by their first names or simply "colored woman," "black lady," etc. Reading those sections had become more and more demeaning and degrading. We were aware that those titles had been applied toward our likeness for far too long. So, the protests against the newspaper began. We stood outside the office where the news was written and printed. We were persistent and determined. There were some who felt that we were fighting a lost cause and that "some things never change." I begged to differ. Naturally, we received backlash from the opposition, but I encouraged everyone to continue the fight. We did. Eventually, I picked up a newspaper, and the "Nigger Page" was gone.

July 6, 1965, marks the day that I was arrested and charged with embezzlement. My mug shot, which can be seen on the front cover of this book, depicts the face of an innocent man awaiting exoneration. I was innocent. I was accused of mishandling the monetary flow of contributions sent to the Dallas County Voters League and utilizing it for my personal gain. As the Dallas County Voters League President, all of the money came directly to me, and there were no outlined policies and procedures. Therefore, money was disbursed as needed. There were many sharecroppers who had lost their homes due to their protesting activities and direct involvement with the movement. There were other hard-working citizens with or without families who, through sacrifice, had lost their homes and jobs as well. Everyone without work was without pay. The school system disapproved of my outspokenness and my participation in the movement, and they reached their peak of disapproval after the Selma to Montgomery march. Below, you will find the initial letter I received to inform me that my wages were being cut. Shortly thereafter, I was fired. I was out of work as an educator for approximately three years.

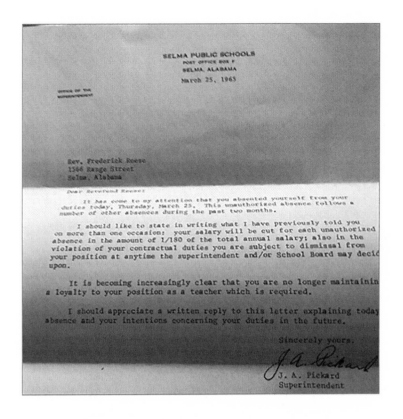

I was not deterred by this letter. I had work to do, and my fight for the people of Selma would continue. The Dallas County Voters League, community volunteers and I set up a food bank and provided toiletry and clothing items with the donations we received. Money was pouring in from many churches and organizations across the country. Church leaders were reaching out to me via telegram or U.S. mail in to determine how they might be of service. I did not allow any money to be deposited in a Selma bank account. In an effort to maintain our privacy, I set up a bank account at Citizens and Trust Bank in Atlanta, Georgia. I made this decision as the President of the Dallas

County Voters League. Some leaders reached out to simply offer prayers and well wishes or to congratulate us on how we were helping others. I was humbled and overwhelmed by the outpouring of expressions of love and support for Selma. Checks were coming in on a daily basis. No amount was too large, and no amount was too small. With the monies received, we were able to enhance our campaign strategies and extend our reach to convince those we weren't able to convince before. Our services equipped us with the ability to make a huge impact on the roster of registered voters. The rolls increased. It is my understanding that during this period, nearly 300 residents were added to the most recent roster.

There was a surge in the number of participants in our literacy classes. It was our duty to plant educational seeds so that our citizens could blossom in the field of voter registration. Marie Foster, Amelia Boynton and I were pivotal in helping engage our "students" in tutoring sessions. We created flash cards and mock tests in order to prepare and equip students with the tools they needed to become registered voters. Many of our students vented their frustrations about their experiences as they approached the registrar's office to register to vote. Test taking can be quite nerve-wrecking, but when preparation meets opportunity, it helps ease the apprehension, and it boosts the confidence one needs in order to succeed. Our students were inspired. As a result, the number of those successfully added to the list of registered voters increased.

It's quite unfortunate that my efforts were being overshadowed by the embezzlement charge I was accused of. I was physically halted due to being placed in jail. Nevertheless, neither the jail cell nor the bars enclosing the cell had the power to stifle my mental thought process. The wheels in my mind are always turning. I'm always thinking of ways to make the lives of others better. In short, I was jailed, released, recharged and ready to continue to fight.

Complete strangers continued to lend their support, sending constant streams of money as a symbol of solidarity toward our small town of Selma. Every amount contributed was appreciated. Every donation received was used wisely. Envelopes were coming in from New York, Illinois and Pennsylvania, to name just a few.

After I was terminated from the school system as a result of my unwavering commitment to the movement, I accepted invites from a number of cities in the country for speaking engagements, dinners, fund raisers, etc. I raised money during my business trips. I spoke with many dignitaries and voiced my concerns and passion for my beloved Selma. I couldn't be a vessel of change if I didn't do everything in my power to bring awareness to the "powers that be." I utilized my time after I was terminated to network and be the voice for Selma. Some members of the SCLC and others in my hometown of Selma felt as though I was operating from a different playing field and had abandoned the grassroots campaign I had begun years ago. But while they were standing still and discussing my whereabouts, I was making strides and campaigning for Selma. Rumors were circulating that not only was I taking money for personal gain, but that I was focusing on politics and had lost sight of the struggle. That assumption was false from every standpoint. I had the opportunity to expand awareness and tap into resources that were not previously available to us. Those with a vendetta against me felt as though they had the ammunition to castigate me and bring me down. I was confident that my defenestration would be short-lived.

Blanchard MacLeod, circuit solicitor, and Wilson Baker, police captain at the time, facilitated the investigation regarding my "illegal activities." Investigators were speaking to donors from all over the country to secure the proof to determine that I had been inappropriately using their donations to pay my mortgage and various other household expenses. But the accusers failed to secure factual information. The Dallas County Voters League, as well as members of the SCLC, were aware that I was granted the same permission as other unemployed residents to receive financial assistance with mortgage payments and household necessities.

I am grateful to J.L. Chestnut, the attorney for the Dallas County Voters League. He expressed that he had known me all of my life, and although he did not agree with many of my recent requests to the city council or demands made to Mayor Joe Smitherman on various projects, Chestnut stated that I was not a "thief." I sincerely appreciate him for speaking up on my behalf, all other differences aside. Chestnut contacted the SCLC to determine if they would provide the financial support needed to defend my case. Initially they seemed hesitant, but eventually they gave in. When I appeared for trial the following year, officers of the Dallas County Voters League testified that I had full permission to use the donations for my personal expenses. There was no need for additional testimony. The case was dismissed! I was cleared of the charges, and my name was no longer tarnished. God knew what I had done. Or in this case, God knew what I had NOT done, and others were able to see that I was innocent as well. *What a mighty God we serve! Thank you, God!*

---

\* Each year on the first weekend in March, the city of Selma celebrates "Jubilee," which commemorates "Bloody Sunday" and the Selma to Montgomery march.

---

*Welcome to Historic Selma*

*Edmund Pettus Bridge*
(Photo by Kathy M. Walters)

*Dallas County Courthouse*
(Photo by Kathy M. Walters)

*Brown Chapel Church*

(Photo by Kathy M. Walters)

*Brown Chapel Church marquee*

(Photo: George Littleton- Auburn University)

*Teachers March Participants*
*Frederick D. Reese, Sarah Carter Craig, Elmyra Martin Smith,*
*Sally Surrency Jackson and Lawrence Huggins (Left to right)*

*Frederick D. Reese (second from right) Martin Luther King,*
*Jr., Coretta Scott King (center)*

(Google Images)

*Frederick D. Reese (far right)*

(Google Images)

*Frederick D. Reese (third from left)*
*Martin Luther King, Jr. (middle)*

174

*Father James Robinson (left center) Coretta Scott King and John Lewis (center) Rev. Dr. Frederick D. Reese (right center)*

(Good Black News)

*Rev. Dr. Frederick D. Reese*

(Google Images)

*Rev. Martin Luther King, Jr. (Left) Coretta Scott King (center) Frederick D. Reese (right)*

(Montgomery Advertiser)

*Frederick D. Reese (right) Martin Luther King, Jr. (left) Ralph David Abernathy (middle) Praying before a march.*

(Google Images)

*Frederick D. Reese (far left) Martin Luther King, Jr. (center)*
(Kathy M. Walters)

*Frederick D. Reese (far left)*
(Google Images)

*Frederick D. Reese (center, holding coat and paperwork)*

(Good Black News)

*Frederick D. Reese (seated), Martin Luther King, Jr.
(podium), Sheyann Webb (foreground)*

(Google Images)

178

*Frederick D. Reese and Alline Reese*

(Family photo)

*Frederick D. Reese (left) Grandson, Alan Reese (right)*
*Faith Reese and Alan Reese Jr. (great-granddaughter and*
*great-grandson of Frederick D. Reese)*

(Family photo)

*Alline Reese and Frederick D. Reese*

(Selma Times Journal)

*Frederick D. Reese (far left) U.S. Representative Terri Sewell (center) Hank Sanders (far right)*

(The Montgomery Advertiser)

*Rev. Dr. Frederick D. Reese*

*Rev. Dr. Frederick D. Reese and Miranda Grass Manley*

Photo by Alecia Howell

Miranda Grass Manley met Rev. Dr. Frederick D. Reese prior to graduating from college. He was recruiting teachers at a job fair. He shared details of "Bloody Sunday", the Edmund Pettus Bridge, and the Selma to Montgomery march. Miranda was not familiar with the history of Selma. Rev. Reese shared a photo where he stood alongside Coretta Scott and Martin Luther King, Jr. He advised Miranda that he was the gentleman holding Coretta's hand, and that he had marched cross the Edmund Pettus Bridge with Martin Luther King, Jr.

Miranda left the job fair that day with a life changing experience. Rev. Reese told Miranda that if she wanted to teach history in Alabama, she needed to learn the history of Selma. Miranda promised him that she would. Though they had a memorable conversation, Miranda never obtained Rev. Reese's name.

Miranda searched for this "mystery man" for 17 years before she found him. Read the entire story and hear how Rev. Reese influenced Miranda's career via YouTube: https://www.youtube.com/watch?v=2RLiPP_95-I&t=90s

*Alan Reese (left), Miranda Grass Manley (Middle) Marvin Reese, Jr. (Right) and 6th, 7th and 8th grade students from Clark-Shaw School of Math and Science, walking across the Edmund Pettus Bridge- photo by Quentin Howard, Manager of MCPSS Television Network*

(Getty Images-Tom Williams)

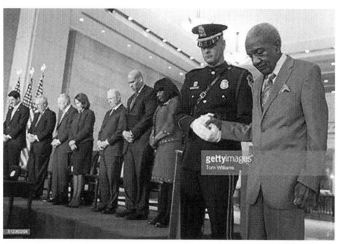

*Rev. Dr. Frederick D. Reese (far right)*

*Phi Beta Sigma Fraternity, Inc.*

(Family photo) Frederick D. Reese

*Phi Beta Sigma Fraternity, Inc.*
*Frederick D. Reese (far left, seated)*

(Family photo)

*F.D. Reese Christian Academy Founder, Pastor Lonnie Anderson/Mt. Pisgah Missionary Baptist Church, Kokomo, Indiana*

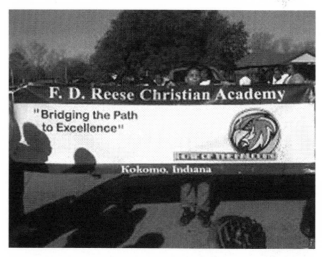

Tina Smiley, of Selma, Alabama saw her lifelong pastor, Rev. Dr. Frederick D. Reese, via an article in American Legacy Magazine. (Below)

When I returned to Selma, Alabama, I reunited with the church where I was baptized. Shortly thereafter, I saw this article in #AmericanLegacyMagazine, titled, 'The Work of the Preachers.' The caption for the picture reads, "Martin Luther King, Jr. (left), Ralph

Abernathy (center), and a supporter kneel in prayer."

REALLY? I wrote American Legacy to have the "supporter" identified. Shortly thereafter, I wrote HJR 231. I will never forget the day Rep. Edward Maul came to tell me that the Resolution had passed. Rep. Maul was extremely happy. On May 28, 2000, we honored Dr. Reese by unveiling "Dr. Frederick D. Reese Parkway". Thank you, Dr. Reese. You taught us well!

"For this corruptible must put on incorruption, and this mortal must put on immortality."

I thank the Lord for Dr. Reese!

*Tina Smiley*
(Tina Smiley's Facebook Page)

(Twitter) #feelselmahistory

*Rev. Dr. Frederick D. Reese*

(Alabama News Network)

(Family Photo)

*Alan Reese*

(Family photo)

(Family photo)

*March4Muscles*
*Frederick D. Reese (center)*

(Family photo)

*March4Muscles*
*Frederick D. Reese (Left) Inside of Club Car*
(Family photo)

*The FD Reese Foundation*

(FD Reese Foundation)

*Rev. Dr. Frederick D. Reese*

FD Reese Foundation

*Marvin Reese, Jr., Demetrius Dower, Alan Reese (left to right)*

(FD Reese Facebook Page)

*FD Reese T-shirt*

(Family photo)

*Alan Reese (grandson) Alline Reese (wife of Rev. Dr. Frederick D. Reese) Marvin Jr. (grandson)- Riverdale High School (Left to right)*

(FD Reese Facebook Page)

*The Reese Home in Selma, Alabama*
*(Listed as an historical site with the Alabama*
*Historical Commission)*

(Kathy M. Walters)

*Montgomery Advertiser- March 22, 2017*

(Kathy M. Walters)

*Rev. Dr. Frederick D. Reese*

(Montgomery Advertiser)

*Frederick D. Reese receiving the Congressional Gold Medal in honor of the Foot Soldiers who marched from Selma to Montgomery in 1965. Medal was introduced by Congresswoman Terri Sewell (U.S. Representative for Alabama's 7th Congressional District. (Pictured in red). Medal was presented by Speaker of the House, Paul Ryan. Also pictured: Representative John Lewis (Far right) Senator Cory Booker (Top right)*

(Google Images)

*Rev. Leodis Strong (left) Rev. Dr. Frederick D. Reese (center) Congresswoman Terri Sewell (right)*

(Photo by: Journalist, Ari Berman)

## Religious Affiliations

Pastor, Ebenezer Baptist Church

Member, Southwest District State Convention

Member, National Baptist Convention

Member, Alabama Baptist State Convention

Moderator, Old Shady Grove District Association

## Education

Alabama State University- B.S. Degree in Secondary Education (Major: Science/ Minor: Mathematics)

Livingston University- M.Ed. in Education, A.A. Specialist Diploma in Administration

Selma University- Doctor of Divinity Degree

## Advanced Study

Liberty University

Liberty Home Bible Institute

University of Alabama

Southern University

Auburn University

## Elementary Training

Clark Elementary School (Selma, Alabama)

High School Training

Knox Academy (Selma, Alabama)

President: Sophomore, Junior, Senior Classes

President: Hi-Y

Secretary, Marshall Patrol

## Honors and Awards (partial listing)

"Who's Who Among Black Americans"

Who's Who in the South and Southwest"

"Teacher of the Year Award", Selma City Teachers Association

"Good Guy Award", Chairman of the United Appeal Division

"The Abraham Lincoln Award" Presented at the National Education Association Convention in Detroit, Michigan (1971)

Appointed as Chairman of the Advisory Council of the Selma to Montgomery National Historic Trail (1998)

Honoree, National Education Association in Washington,

DC- Annual Martin Luther King Jr. Commemorative Program (2009)

Congressional Gold Medal – Emancipation Hall on Capitol Hill, Washington, DC (2016)

## (2000)

U.S. Route 80 in Selma Alabama was named the Frederick D. Reese Parkway (3 mile stretch of the highway)

The F.D. Reese Christian Academy in Kokomo, Indiana dedicated to Rev. Dr. Frederick D. Reese

(The school's motto is:" We are proud to be named after a living civil rights legend")

## Professional Leadership/Affiliations

Member, Economic Opportunity Board

President, Wilcox Teachers Association

Member, Personnel Committee, EOB

Member, Board of Directors, Good Samaritan Hospital

President, Selma-Dallas Black Leadership Council

Member, Selma City Council, 12 years

Candidate for the office of Mayor in 1984

Member, Board of Directors, Carver Branch YMCA

Chairman, Wilcox County Teachers Planning Committee

Assistant Principal, Wilcox County Training School

Instructor, Science and Mathematics, R.B. Hudson High School

Chairman, Discipline Committee, R. B. Hudson High School

President, Campus Society of Musicians, Alabama State University

Assistant Director, Southern Region, Phi Beta Sigma Fraternity, Inc.

Member, Alabama Education Association

Member, National Association of Secondary Principals

Member, National Education Association

Administrative Assistant to the Superintendent of Education, Selma City Schools

Principal, Selma High School

Principal, Eastside Junior High School

Assistant Principal, Eastside Junior High School

Member, Council for Leaders in Alabama Schools

Member, Association for Supervision and Curriculum Development

President, Gamma Beta Chapter, Phi Beta Sigma Fraternity, Inc.

State Director, Bigger and Better Business, Phi Beta Sigma Fraternity, Inc.

President, Pan Hellenic Council, Alabama State University

First Black President, Selma Education Association

## Political Influence

*Instrumental in the hiring process of the first Black Deputy in the Dallas County Sheriff's Department in Selma

*Led the fight to ban smoking in the City Council Chambers in Selma

*As City Council Member, led the process in the renaming of Sylvan Street to Martin Luther King, Jr. Street in Selma

*Led the fight to hire the first Black policeman and first black Director of the Neighborhood Services Center in Selma

"Frederick D. Reese vs. Cobbs & Other"- Court case concerning the discrimination against jurors within the court system.

Outcome: "Federal Court ruled that jury boxes must be emptied and non-discriminatory systems be used in the selections of citizens to serve on jury duty." (Nondescript Fact Sheet)

---

**More than 200 plaques and certificates for Outstanding Leadership (Religion, Civil Rights and Education)

*Rev. Dr. Frederick D. Reese*

(Selma Times Journal)

# UNSUNG HEROES

"*I*f there is no struggle, there is no progress."
Frederick Douglass

Long after the marches, jail stays and beatings, I can't recall a time when I would see the late Rev. Hosea Williams and he wouldn't inquire, "When is your book coming out?" I had visited the thought in my mind and had begun to document highlights of my life, but I didn't set a deadline or anticipate becoming an author right away. I must admit that it wasn't a priority at the time, as my focus was set on the movement and getting things done. But I'm a firm believer that while some things happen as we plan them, all things happen in God's time, and only when He wants them to happen. So I'd respond to Hosea, "In God's time, Hosea. In God's time."

Years after I had served as a pastor, principal, educator, great-grandfather, grandfather and husband, many people from near and far, as well as those in my hometown of Selma, often advised me that my accolades were by no means commensurate with that of the more celebrated civil rights leaders I have protested with and served alongside during the civil rights era. Although I have marched hand in hand, fought beside, held private conversations with, prayed with and for, and knelt beside many civil rights leaders who were in the forefront during those times, some of whom are prominent figures today, I hold no animosity, envy or resentment for not being nationally or globally recognized as they have been. Popularity was never a part of my plan. My purpose for my fight was driven by my passion to participate in the political process. Nothing more. Above all, I feel humbled to know that I fought for the masses. My focus was set on the movement, not the acknowledgment. I couldn't fathom the notion of standing by idly. That's not how I was raised. I wanted to serve Selma by lending a hand and using my voice wherever and whenever I could.

As a result of my popularity, or lack thereof, I've met people within Selma and beyond who have requested answers to their many questions. These are the people who know me, as well as those who may have simply met me. Upon hearing of my accomplishments or running across a photo from the civil rights era, or after learning that I received the Medal of Honor, they are passionate about my contributions as well as the contributions of other unsung heroes. Both the young and the more seasoned individuals have been unrelenting with their concerns, and I don't take it lightly:

*Can you tell me why your name isn't included in my history books?*

*Why have others been on the national forefront, but those who lived, breathed and died for civil rights, right here in Selma, are unheard of?*

*Are you the man in the photo with Dr. Martin Luther King, Jr.? I never knew that that was you!*

*How could you have done so much and have been recognized so little, yet you still remain so humble?*

If Hosea were here today, I could finally let him know that my story is written and my book has been released to the world. Hosea stands out when I think of the number of times I was posed with the question and the number of people who approached me with their thoughts on those individuals who should be properly noted for their sacrifice in Selma.

It seems that the entire world was glued to either their television sets or their transistor radios on March 7, 1965, during Bloody Sunday. Millions witnessed the live accounts of senseless brutality on the streets of our small town. The eyes of the world were watching Selma. Some watched with fear, rage and sadness, while many others watched with sheer joy and excitement. Others sent up cheers and held the violence in high regard, all of which represent the reactions of a truly divided nation. Then, two weeks later, the world listened to the speech commonly known as "How Long, Not Long" by Dr. Martin Luther King, Jr. following the Selma to Montgomery march.

The individuals who were making headlines in the news were known all around the world. There were some who were placed in history books, and there are those who remain household names today. Many can be found in photos that have circulated around the world. "Rev. Reese, I've seen you in a photo with..."

"Rev. Reese, isn't this you in this photo with…" To this day, I smile at them, nod my head, and answer, "Yes, it is. That's me." They continue to ask questions, because they do not understand. To the many others posing questions about my obscurity… please allow me to unpack a five-word explanation: God knows what I did. And while that response remains as one of my frequently used mantras, it is my added duty to pay homage to the foot soldiers and those who fought for years, lending both passion and compassion, sacrificing so much of themselves in the fight for justice, and yet, they too are unnoticed, unknown and unrecognized for their contributions.

Many have encouraged me to "call out" those who may have accepted accolades that belonged to me. Others have suggested that I identify those who entered Selma, made a name for themselves and moved on. I'm responding to those inquiries in this book so that I may address it one final time. I will respond by saying that neither then nor now will I choose to dim anyone's light in order to brighten my glow. Those who received popularity earned it in their own way, and to others who may have received accolades that were due others, I must express that I love them all the same. And if I may alter my mantra, I do so by saying, God knows what THEY did. Bitterness is a choice. And I choose to not live my life in toxicity. There's enough darkness in the world for all of us to emit our own individual light. It's my hope to shine the light on the unsung heroes, the ones who were unnoticed in the foreground, those who are due the accolades they have long been denied. End of story.

During the civil rights era, social media was nonexistent.

Without documentation at this juncture, many important historical facts and figures will continue to be fragmented or eradicated altogether. My hope is that the historical details of the civil rights movement in Selma be recorded with accuracy, inclusion and completion. There are many broken links in Selma's history, and my goal is to mend a portion that is broken and pay homage to the fearless foot soldiers so that their contributions to the movement are acknowledged.

⁓

Struggle, bloodshed, tears and sacrifice loomed over the rivers, banks and bridges of Selma and surrounding cities long before those atrocities of the past were witnessed by the world. The Dallas County Voters League had been a driving force for change and was very successful in broadening awareness and educating blacks concerning their right to vote in the early years.

I wish to make special mention of Amelia and Sam Boynton. As far back as the late 1930s, Amelia Boynton became a registered voter, and alongside her first husband, Sam, they dedicated themselves to encouraging blacks in Selma to reach for the stars and refrain from allowing oppressors to block their achievements. Amelia spread the word about the importance of exercising the right to vote, and Sam encouraged entrepreneurship. Both stressed the importance of education. They owned several businesses in Selma, and together, they stood for and marched for the rights of those who were disenfranchised, mistreated and otherwise overlooked. They helped to resuscitate a dying NAACP in Selma. Sam Boynton was president of the Dallas

County Voters League, which was founded by Charles J. Adams in the 1920s. The Boyntons were leaders in the community. They worked hard, and their contributions should be recognized.

After Sam's passing, Amelia continued to advocate for the importance of voting rights. She would stand outside the courthouse in an attempt to vouch for potential voters, she continued marching for the rights of others, and she was nationally recognized as the woman who was severely beaten on Bloody Sunday. Amelia Boynton passed away in 2015.

The world needs to know that the blueprint was created and the foundation was poured long before some of the more popular leaders stepped foot onto Selma's soil. It is our duty to pay homage and honor to some of those who are seldom mentioned or failed to be recognized at all. Many thanks to the Boyntons, who were leaders and servants, and who helped to pave the way for so many!

# SELMA REMEMBERS

*Assisted Selma residents with registering to vote as early as 1930's/1940's*
*Amelia Boynton*

(Google Images)

## The Courageous Eight

*(Old Depot Museum) Selma, Alabama*

*Rev. James Galloway- Civil Rights Leader.*
*Rev. James Galloway helped to organize a trip to Ipswich,*
*Massachusetts, and 36 Selma students were chosen to participate in*
*the voter registration drive.*

(Kathryn Galloway)

*Annie Lee Cooper*
*Annie Lee Cooper is known for "punching" Sheriff Jim Clark in the*
*jaw after he struck her with a billy club.*
*Annie Lee Cooper was standing in line at the Dallas County*
*Courthouse in Selma. She was attempting to register to vote)*

(Google Images)

*Betty Mae Fikes*
*Betty Mae Fikes sang with the SNCC Freedom singers. She often sang in jail cells and mass meetings. She was arrested numerous times while protesting against injustice. She is a former student from R.B. Hudson High School*

*Sheyann Webb*
*Then and Now- Sheyann Webb is famously known as the youngest marcher on Bloody Sunday. Sheyann was only 8 years old.*

(Google Images)

*Jimmie Lee Jackson*
*Jimmie Lee Jackson was a deacon at his church. He was killed by a State Trooper during a peaceful protest in Marion, Alabama.*

(Google Images)

*Viola Liuzza.*
*Viola Liuzza was killed by the KKK for transporting a black civil rights worker back to Selma after the Selma to Montgomery march.*

(Google Images)

*4 Little girls killed by member of the KKK*
*Selma sit-in (1965) (Wikipedia) (Google Images)*
*Top left: Addie Mae Collins (14)*
*Top right: Cynthia Wesley (14)*
*Bottom left: Denise McNair (11)*
*Bottom Right: Carole Robertson*

*16th Street Baptist Church Bombing- September 15, 1963*

# APRIL 5, 2018-

(Selma Times Journal)

O DEATH, WHERE IS THY STING? O GRAVE, WHERE IS THY VICTORY? The sting of death is sin; and the strength of sin is in the law. But thanks be to God, which giveth us the victory through our Lord Jesus Christ. Therefore, my beloved brethren, be ye steadfast, unmovable, always abounding in the work of the Lord, forasmuch as you know that your labor is not in vain in the Lord.

1 Corinthians 15:55-58 (KJV)

Rev. Dr. Frederick D. Reese departed this life and earned his heavenly wings on Thursday, April 5, 2018. When I received the call from his grandson, Alan Reese, I imagined he might be calling to provide additional information I'd requested for the book, or that he was merely checking to see how I was doing, so I gently slid my finger across the "Accept" option on my phone and cheerfully answered.

"Hi, Alan! How are you?" I chimed.

"I'm doing fine, Kathy. I just wanted to call and let you know that my grandfather made his transition today, and I wanted you to hear it from me."

The sound waves carrying Alan's voice were that of peace and calm. I was engaged in the serene flow of Alan's words, because anyone close to Alan and the Reese family knows that he loved his grandfather to the core of his being, and from the bottom of his heart. The content of our phone conversation was so unexpected that I had become numb and speechless. I had met with Rev. Reese, Mrs. Alline Reese and other members of the family on several occasions while gathering information for this book. They were so gracious, so genuine, and so kind. In many ways, it seemed as if I had known these jewels all of my life.

As Alan shared more details of his grandfather's passing, I furrowed my brows and closed my eyes. I mentally replayed one of the last conversations that I would ever have with Rev. Reese one Sunday as we sat in the dining room of Alan and his beautiful wife Kimberly's home. I'd asked Rev. Reese questions about his life and his upbringing. I also received feedback from Mrs. Reese and their daughter, Christa. I was intrigued. Toward the close of our conversation, I had expressed to Rev. Reese that once he holds the first copy of his book in his hands, it will be one of the most exuberant, rewarding indescribable feelings that he's ever experienced. I remembered how his lips curled into a slight smile and how he looked at me with a nondescript expression. I couldn't read his emotions, because he didn't say a word. Nevertheless, it made me ponder.

"Kathy, are you okay?" I opened my eyes as I attempted to dislodge the reality that Rev. Reese was really gone. I switched the phone from my left ear and over to the right ear, looking down at my feet as I paced the floor. "Alan, I am so sorry. This is such a shock. I just can't believe this. Are you okay? How is everyone?" I rambled. Alan informed me that everyone was maintaining, and he advised me to stay encouraged and keep doing what I was doing. He went on to say that God had called his grandfather home, and that Rev. Reese is in a much better place.

"Therefore, we are always confident, knowing that, whilst we are at home in the body, we are absent from the Lord :( For we walk by faith, not by sight :) We are confident, I say, and willing rather to be absent from the body, and to be present with the Lord." (2 Corinthians 5:6-8 KJV)

"We're going to carry out his legacy, Kathy. Everything is going to be fine." I stopped pacing and lifted my head up. Hiding my emotions from Alan, or so I thought, I pressed the mute button on my phone and remained silent. I gingerly wiped the tears that were flowing freely from my eyes as I attempted to pull myself together. Confirming that I had clearly failed to conceal

215

my sadness, Alan began to speak. "Be strong, Kathy. Thanks again, and I really appreciate you." Relieved and unaware that I had been holding my breath for quite some time, I freely exhaled. "No. Thank you, Alan. I'm so honored to be a part of this project. And again, I'm so sorry. My condolences to you and the family."

The Celebration of Life service for Rev. Dr. Frederick D. Reese took place on Friday, April 13, 2018, at 11 a.m. Even the mourners who arrived early found the parking area nearly filled when they turned onto the street leading to the church. Attendees were maneuvering their vehicles to create a parking spot wherever they could space. The main level of the sanctuary, as well as the balcony, quickly filled to capacity in a relatively large house of worship. Some guests remained in the vestibule, and they didn't mind standing as long as they were able to pay their respects to this great man in any way they could. To graciously accommodate the crowd, ushers began setting up chairs down the aisles of the sanctuary, which allowed those who were previously standing a comfortable place to sit. Everyone was operating in decency and order. "Borrowing" and paraphrasing one of Rev. Dr. Frederick D. Reese's famous sayings, I must add that everyone exhibited proper decorum.

Held at his beloved Ebenezer Baptist Church, located at 1548 F.D. Reese Street in Selma, Alabama, where he served as pastor for 50 years, the service for Rev. Dr. Frederick D. Reese was finally underway. Soft music filled the sanctuary throughout the morning. In attendance, and replicating the famous attire for which Rev. Hosea Williams was famously known, were members of the SCLC. With erected flags and a stance with full salute, the men and women, wearing blue overalls and red bandanas neatly and uniformly tied around their necks, stood on either side of the church's entryway. As the family entered the sanctuary, the congregation stood. The atmosphere within the sanctuary generated a sense of respect, reverence and richness. Every speaker approaching the platform had a special relationship with Rev. Dr. Frederick D. Reese. The depth of his impact resonated through their words, songs and tributes. His daughter, Minister Valerie Harris, Director of Choirs at Miles College, directed the ensemble as they sang two of her father's favorite songs, "*I Need Thee Every Hour*" and "*It Is Well.*" She also shared loving thoughts about her father and reflected upon his love for Handel's Messiah. Daughter Minister Christa Reese penned a beautiful poetic tribute entitled, *Farewell, My Wonderful Father.* Grandson Alan Reese, CEO of the FD Reese Foundation, spoke warm, heartfelt words about his grandfather, which led to a standing ovation. Grandson Marvin Reese, Jr. graced the congregation with his God-given, melodious voice as he sang "*Precious Lord,*" which brought both tears and expressions of praise throughout the pews of his grandfather's church. The President of the FD Reese Foundation, Demetrius Dower, astutely shared knowledge about the movement and provided much-needed awareness about the FD Reese Foundation. A dear friend of Rev. Dr. Frederick D. Reese, Pastor R.L. Patterson of Abyssinia Baptist Church, Ensley, Birmingham, Alabama, spoke about an agreement the two of them had discussed, and one which he never imagined he would truly have to fulfill. They agreed that whoever was the last survivor would deliver the other's eulogy.

And Pastor R.L. Patterson delivered a wonderful eulogy that evoked deep emotions in the congregation as he honored his end of the agreement. Professor Maurice Hobson, a well-spoken historian at Georgia State University, shared reflections of his personal experience with Rev. Dr. Frederick D. Reese. Bishop Theo Bailey of Christ Temple Deliverance Church of Birmingham, Alabama, blessed everyone with a heartfelt prayer. Soloist Bonita G. Conley embodied the voice of an angel as she sang, *"How Beautiful are the Feet of Them,"* by G.F. Handel. Rev. James Perkins, Jr., Rev. Dr. Frederick D. Reese's successor, mentee and a man of God whom Dr. Reese was quite fond of, provided gracious reflections. A resolution was eloquently read by an educator and former student of Rev. Dr. Frederick D. Reese, Althelstein Johnson. Pastor Charles Burns of Morning Star Baptist Church, Demopolis Alabama, and Pastor Lonnie Anderson of Mt. Pisgah Baptist Church, Kokomo, Indiana, and founder of the F.D. Reese Christian School, provided scripture from the Old Testament and the New Testament, respectively. Warm expressions of gratitude were provided by the U.S. Representative for Alabama's 7th Congressional District, Congresswoman Terri A. Sewell. Additionally, a video presentation was shown and a song was presented by the beloved Ebenezer Baptist Church Choir. The Celebration of Life service for Frederick D. Reese was heartfelt, warm and befitting for such a peaceful but strong force, whose contributions truly left an indelible mark on so many people's lives in his beloved Selma.

One might wonder why this chapter is entitled April 5, 2018-, with a hyphen at the end. Usually when someone passes, the hyphen is displayed between the date the individual was born and the date of their transition. Well, here's the explanation: Rev. Dr. Frederick D. Reese, without question, parted this life on April 5, 2018. However, the hyphen placed after his transition date reflects continuity. Through the way in which he lived his life, the way he loved, the way he stood for what was right, the vast difference he made to individuals and to the voting rights movement, and subsequently through the impact he had on Selma, the hyphen delineates the legacy of Rev. Dr. Frederick D. Reese's contributions, which is certain to live on for generations. Rev. Dr. Frederick D. Reese was a humble man. Alan Reese often speaks about a time while studying Black History in grade school. His class was reading a book that included a photo of civil rights leaders, and Alan immediately noticed that his grandfather's photograph was included on one of the pages. "Hey, this is my granddad!" he told his classmates. No one believed him. "This really is my granddad!" he exclaimed. He confidently advised his teacher and his class that he would prove that the man in the photo, though uncaptioned, was truly his granddad. And that he did. Shortly thereafter, Alan proudly brought his granddad, Rev. Dr. Frederick D. Reese, to speak to his class! From that day forth, it was placed on Alan's heart and embedded in his drive to circumvent similar occurrences in the future. Moreover, Alan's mission was to ensure that his children and his children's children and the world would know exactly who his granddad was, educating as many as possible about Rev. Dr. Frederick D. Reese's contributions to the voting rights movement and how it all unfolded in Selma, Alabama! Alan's ultimate goal is to secure the integrity and the proper acknowledgement of historical facts for generations to come. And the FD Reese Foundation is making certain of it. The Reese family is making strides to encapsulate the spirit and contributions of their beloved Frederick D. Reese in the purest form. Therefore, it is befitting and imperative to highlight the FD Reese Foundation and share the concepts of the "true foundation" upon which it is being built.

The FD Reese Foundation is commissioned as a resource to nurture the minds of youth. The foundation is making strides to spark change in the community and to "honor Dr. Frederick Douglas Reese's legacy through practical education methods in order to make a global impact on humanity. The foundation strives to address the disenfranchisement of students in some of the nation's underserved and impoverished communities to build universal leaders." In addition, the foundation "seeks to raise awareness of critical issues facing the community through culturally relevant education services and scholarship opportunities." (www.fdreesefoundation.org).

Currently, there are three F.D. Reese scholarships: the F.D. Reese Essay Grant, which is open to high school students; the Alma Mater F.D. Reese Scholarship, which is extended to high school and college students who aspire to attend Alabama State University; and the HBCU F.D. Reese Scholarship, which is open to high school and college students who are attending historically black colleges and universities. The F.D. Reese Foundation and the resources it provides are designed to bridge the gap between those aspiring to further their education and those who also require assistance to achieve their goals. Frederick D. Reese held a high regard for education, and the foundation's goal is to ensure that students who desire the benefits of an education will not be denied the opportunity of realizing their goals.

As mentioned earlier in this book, whenever Rev. Dr. Frederick D. Reese was asked how it felt to be unrecognized or to be identified merely as the "unnamed gentleman" in numerous photos that have been circulated around the world, alongside more prominently recognized civil rights leaders, he would always respond, "God knows what I did." He was beyond humble. His quiet yet strong charismatic presence bred humility. Although he received upward of 200 honors and awards, he never boasted. He never treated anyone as less than himself. Many who knew him spoke highly of his character. Although he is no longer with us in the physical realm to bask in the kind words and achievements highlighted in this book, I would like to share personal accounts from a few of the many who knew him well. Their expressions, including a January 11, 1964, congratulatory telegram from Martin Luther King, Jr., allow us to fully understand what Rev. Dr. Frederick D. Reese meant to them, how he affected their lives, and how he encouraged others to stand and fight the good fight. Each witnessed the great qualities embodied by a great man, who was courageous and filled with the love of God, and who was also admired and respected by so many. Below are the stories, as told through their eyes:

*F.D. Reese was my Daddy, and when I think of all the things that he did and how he stood for right, whether in the community or the educational or church arena, I'm just proud* to be his daughter. My Daddy was definitely a disciplinarian. He was the one who carried out the discipline with a belt or whatever he deemed necessary to help us understand that he was serious about whatever we were being disciplined for. Daddy did not play around about education, home chores or church activities. Whatever we were a part of, he expected us to do our best, and he "encouraged" us.

I never felt pressure as the daughter of a civil rights leader, because I was busy trying to be who I was and the person Daddy encouraged me to be. Sometimes I felt this pressure as the daughter of a pastor because we were a part of Ebenezer Baptist Church, where Daddy pastored and everybody watched everything we did as if we were under a microscope. Maybe I sometimes wanted to do something that was a little out of the norm, but I was always conscious that I was "Rev. Reese's daughter." What I began to understand was that even though Daddy was "the name," we were a part of him, so there was some responsibility that went along with being his daughter, and I understood that.

In coping with the death of both of my brothers from muscular dystrophy, we were taught about death from an early age, and probably because our brothers were not promised a long life, death was a discussion that happened a lot in our home. Not morbid talk, but just life talk that included Mama, Daddy or Frederick Jr. and Alan not always being here on this earth. It was difficult to lose two brothers, but we stood on what we had been taught in the WORD, and we walked through it like a family that has been taught and knows that life had to continue. We would tell stories and laugh and talk about Bro (Frederick Jr.) and Alan, and this helped us in the healing process. I don't think growing up in the Reese household was any different than growing up in another household. We had chores, we practiced our musical lessons, we took care of our brothers, and we did what other normal families do.

In sharing what I appreciate about my Daddy, The Messiah in particular was something that Daddy started in the 1970s, and I have been one of the only musicians who has played this classical work every year since its inception. There were other musicians, but it seemed to always fall to me, and Daddy depended on me to know my music. There was one specific chorus that was quite difficult for a 14-year-old, my age at the time, and Daddy called on that piece in rehearsal. I had been practicing but I wasn't ready yet. But... my Daddy was not going to be outdone, and he informed me in his FD Reese voice that I was going to play it and that was it. At the time, it did not feel good, and I cried, but my Daddy could see what was in me, and for that I am eternally grateful. This reflects a pivotal point in my life on which I now look back on and laugh and smile.

I want the world to know that my Daddy was a GREAT man and a man of integrity and character. He taught us to be the same, and I want the world to know that I loved MY DADDY and I'm proud to be called his daughter. I remember during the interview process for my present position at Miles College, President French asked, "Are you the daughter of *civil rights leader F.D. Reese from Selma? Really?" I proudly answered, "Yes, I AM!!"*

**Valerie Reese-Harris,**
**Daughter of Rev. Dr. Frederick D. Reese**

*There aren't many men in Selma like Frederick D. Reese. He was a "complete man." When he spoke, his presence demanded attention. I've never seen him dressed in anything other than a suit and tie. Some of us have seen him cut the grass in a suit! The way he spoke, and his vocabulary...*

*Rev. Reese was my principal at Selma High School. I can remember hearing him stand in the hallway and say, "We will move through the hallway swiftly and expeditiously." He would also say we were to have "proper auditorium decorum." He reminded me of Joe Clark, the principal played by Morgan Freeman, in the movie, "Lean on me."*

*Rev. Reese always thanked God. He was selfless and never self-promoting. He would often say that he was given an opportunity and that he was a vessel.*

*Rev. Reese always spoke positive thoughts. He was never ruffled, he never raised his voice and he never tooted his own horn.*

*In 1992, the Selma High School football team won the 1st Area Championship. Everyone was in the gym dancing, celebrating and having a good time. Blasting throughout the entire gym was music by the group, The 2 Live Crew." The girls and boys were dancing to the group's hit song, "Pop that Coochie." We didn't know Rev. Reese was at the school. We* thought he was gone. But out of nowhere, he stopped the music. When the music stopped, everyone stopped dancing. You could hear a pin drop. Rev. Reese grabbed the microphone and said, "This is not proper decorum, and there will be no popping of the coochie!" All of the students were shocked, but inside we were laughing because we didn't know he knew what coochie was!

**Demetrius Dower, President of the FD Reese Foundation, Family Member, and Former Student**

I met Rev. Reese as a school-aged child. We lived in the same neighborhood, and he was my 8th grade math teacher. He was a good teacher. Rev. Reese was very kind, and he cared about all of his students. During that era, teachers cared for you and prepared you for life in whatever you set out to do. They encouraged you to be the best that you could be. It was my first year in high school, and I needed to go to my locker and then to the restroom before going to class. Shortly after I exited the restroom, I heard the tardy bell. I was officially late for class! Rev. Reese approached me in the hallway and took my name down on a slip of paper. I can't put into words the embarrassment I felt as I heard my name being read over the intercom for the entire school to hear! But none of that changed my attitude toward him. Rev. Reese was always respectful, and he was always fair. All of the students and teachers respected him, and so did I.

**Carrie DeYampert Grider**
**Former Student**

*I am the former Secretary for Rev. Reese. Rev. Reese was very easy to work for. Although I was his employee and worked for him, he would send out his own correspondence, and he would always help straighten up his office. He was hands on, and once he made you aware of what needed to be done, he would leave you alone and would later come back. He was a pastor, administrator and a very caring father figure to the students. He was a good listener, and he spoke quietly. He served as pastor during the time he served on the City Council. Rev. Reese was instrumental in the decision to hire me by Mayor Smitherman in City Hall. I was the only black employee in the Tax and License Department. As a matter of fact, I was the first black to work in the Tax and License Department. I worked there for five years before returning to the school system. Again, I worked for Rev. Reese when he was the principal of Selma High School! Rev. Reese performed the marriage ceremony for my husband, Eddie, and I 44 years ago, and he also ordained Eddie as a deacon for Ebenezer Baptist Church. Rev. Reese baptized our three children and our two grandchildren. He performed the marriage ceremonies of one of our children and one of our grandchildren. I believe it may have been one of the last wedding ceremonies he performed.*

**Caroline Robinson**
**Former Secretary**

*Dr. Reese was my pastor for 35 years. He performed the marriage ceremony for Cynthia and me 33 years ago. He* licensed me as a minister in 2010, and he ordained me as a Baptist minister in the year 2012. Upon his retirement in 2015, he recommended me to succeed him as pastor of Ebenezer Baptist Church in Selma, Alabama.

When Dr. Reese ran for City Council, my father served as his campaign manager. When Dr. Reese ran for mayor of Selma, I served as his campaign manager, and subsequently, when I ran for mayor, both Dr. Reese and my father served as my campaign managers. My association with Dr. Reese runs deep and wide.

I've been asked if I felt any pressure upon having to "fill the shoes" of Rev. Reese. I can answer that by stating that I felt both pressured and prepared. Pressured, following his 50-year legacy, yet prepared because he trained me well. Rev. Reese allowed me to perform all pastoral duties for three years prior to his retirement. After his retirement, the humility he demonstrated by submitting to my leadership was extraordinary. Total submission and total fellowship, leaving no room for doubt among congregants as to who was/is pastor. Because of his demonstrated wisdom, in my opinion, our transition could not have gone any smoother.

I've been blessed to have a biological father, James Perkins, Sr., and I had as a spiritual father F.D. Reese. Both were persistent and focused in their missions and consistent in their faith. I say without hesitation they have taught me, by example, that "patience, persistence, and prayer produce opportunities to perform."

Rev. Reese definitely impacted my life. I know firsthand

*of the attacks with the intent to destroy him, the lies with the intent to discredit him, the skullduggery with the intent to demoralize him; yet to watch him endure it all and to see his victory... to outlive most who undermined him, has been a deep and impactful lesson that I draw from daily. I describe Rev. Reese as a complete package ... spiritually, mentally and physically solid.*

*When asked to share a funny story, one thing that Rev. Reese did that I refuse to emulate is... I will not suit up EVERY morning. I cannot understand it and will not do it! That's final!*

*I discuss Rev. Reese and the movement throughout Selma with my children, my grandchildren and all who are void of the knowledge and wisdom the movement holds. As for how I feel to be a part of such an important piece of history? Humbled. And for that, I say, "To God be the glory!" The one thing I want the world to know about Rev. Reese is that his life and his legacy are worth studying.*

### Rev. James Perkins, First Black Mayor of Selma, Alabama, Senior Pastor, Ebenezer Baptist Church

*Rev. Reese was such a powerhouse in our community. You couldn't grow up in Selma, Alabama as I did and not know of him, either as an educator, a pastor or civil rights icon. He was truly a renaissance man. Not only was he the pastor of a well-known church in our community, but he was also the first black principal of Selma High School. I graduated from Selma High School. His son, Marvin, and I were in* elementary school together. So I feel like I've always known the Reese family, and I've always known Rev. Reese as a larger than life giant in our community for a host of reasons.

Both my parents were educators. My dad was the high school basketball coach, and my mom was the high school librarian. You couldn't be a black teacher in Selma and not know the power of Rev. Reese and the legacy that he left in his wake. He was a living legend. I grew up hearing my mom telling stories of how Rev. Reese was the first to invite Dr. King to come to Selma. He was the head of the Dallas County Teachers Association and also the head of the Dallas County Voters League, and he was an amazing man who was truly ahead of his time. He was a very powerful figure. I never saw him without a hat. He was always immaculately dressed. He had a booming voice, and he was an amazing presence in our community. He was well respected. He walked by example. To grow up and hear all of the stories about the various things he did, it was not surprising to me that he was a part of the Courageous Eight or that he was a very influential person during the voting rights movement, and that it was he who penned the letter that invited them to come to Selma.

I always felt that he never got his due. When I was lucky enough to be elected as Alabama's first black congresswoman, I made it one of my passions to always nominate him year after year for the Presidential Medal of Freedom because I felt you had to give folks their roses when they're alive. I was one of many sending in names and support letters, and

*I knew I couldn't make the decision for the President, but I also knew that I could do what I could in my own wheelhouse within Congress to honor the legacy of Rev. Reese and the foot soldiers. I was honored to introduce and get passed the Congressional Gold Medal for the foot soldiers who marched from Selma to Montgomery. I told Congressman Lewis that he was the natural, if Congress was going to give a gold medal to foot soldiers, and that he would be the likely choice to accept the medal, but I also told him that I grew up in Selma and I really would be honored if he'd let me give the special honor to Rev. Reese. He was so gracious and said, "But of course you would want Rev. Reese to accept it!" Rev. Reese did a great job accepting the Congressional Gold Medal, which was presented by the Speaker of the House, Paul Ryan. I was honored to host him, his wife and his daughter during their time in Washington.*

*I believe part of my job is to protect and to further the legacy of the 7th Congressional District of the foot soldiers, both known and unknown.*

*What I learned from Rev. Reese is the importance of how one person can make a difference in a community. He didn't speak to merely speak. He spoke with such authority. He was a towering image of a man. He was a man of few words, but when he spoke, everyone listened. I learned the importance of speaking up, and when you see injustice, you speak out. He wasn't afraid to fight. He was grounded in his faith, which gave him the temerity, the audacity, to fight. He was grounded in the fact that he believed fervently in God above,* and he believed in God's protection and grace. He wasn't just an educated man, but he was a man of God.

I have the utmost respect for Rev. Reese. Being in his presence was always a treat. And I know that every day I get to walk the halls of Congress because of his courage, bravery and audacity; to challenge the establishment, knowing that right was on his side. It's an honor every day to know that I do what I do because of the sacrifices of others, and it only makes you want to do better. Rev. Reese laid the foundation of what became the voting rights movement, and I want him to have his place in history.

**Terri Sewell, Alabama's First Black Congresswoman (U.S. Representative for Alabama's 7th Congressional District)**

My husband and I moved to Selma in 1967. Rev. Reese was a community leader, and we would attend meetings together. I worked with Rev. Reese as part of the Selma Dallas Leadership Council. I worked with strategies and took the minutes during the meetings. Rev. Reese was the principal at East Side Middle School. He later came to serve of principal at Selma High School. From there, he became the Assistant Superintendent of Education for Selma City Schools until he retired. I worked very closely with Rev. Reese. I served as the Head Librarian Media Specialist and Student Council Advisor at Selma High School. I played a big role at the school. I was his "go-to" person. If he needed something done, he knew I was the one who would take care of it. I successfully chaired many committees under his administration. He was an awesome leader. He would delineate what needed to be done, and then he would retreat and leave you to complete the task, utilizing your creativity. He would never hover over you. Instead, he had faith in your work. He entrusted you to do a good job. After you completed the task and presented it to him, he would check it. The kids loved him, and the teachers did as well. He was not harsh. He was a leader with discernment. If he knew you couldn't do something, he would help you. And he would help you privately. He would never embarrass you. At Selma High School, he was compared to a "granddaddy" because of the love and compassion he demonstrated to his students. He respected his students. He was very articulate and had wisdom galore. He was a man of courage, conviction and integrity. Once he made up his mind about something, he did not waver. He would look someone straight in the eyes when he spoke to them. He did not beat around the bush. He was very concise in his speech. His eyes were piercing. It seemed as though Rev. Reese could see through the souls of others. He pulled the best out of you. I believe he could tell if you were lying. I always told him the truth.

A City Council position became available around the early 1990s because a member was resigning and leaving Selma. The council announced that someone would be appointed to fill the position for the remaining year and a half left by the outgoing member. The council felt that there was no need to have an election. I stood from the floor and challenged them. Why? I refused to allow that to happen. I challenged them to the point where they had to cough up the money and hold an election. I ran against the white man they were going to appoint, and I lost by only a few votes. I was always told that if you only lost by a few votes the first time, the chances of winning were greater on the second go round. So, after his year and half was over, and when it was time for another election, I ran again against that same gentleman in the general election in 1993. I ran with fervor. I won the election. I broke the ice and became the first African American woman elected to the City Council of Selma, Alabama. I held that seat for nearly 12 years. I felt as if I had to step up and do my fair share. We each had a role to play.

People fail to give credit to Rev. Reese for all he has done. He was a hero in his hometown and never received the credit due him. I would like to see him recognized as the eminent leader of the civil rights movement in Selma. I know that Dr. King was invited to Selma, but Rev. Reese laid the groundwork for the movement in Selma. Rev. Reese never sought the spotlight.

After years of working alongside Rev. Reese, serving and helping to plan strategies, I realize that he set so many find examples. And when we saw his courage, it gave us courage. Rev. Reese was a born leader!

**Nancy Sewell, First Black Female elected for City Council of Selma, Alabama**

*I have known Dr. Reese since I was about 10 years old. My mom was the Secretary at one of the schools where he served as Principal. When my day ended at the elementary school, I would go over to the middle school and remain with my mom until she got off work. So I had the opportunity to see him at the school sometimes.*

*Dr. Reese was a very humble and quiet soul. However, the few times I visited his church to hear him preach, I realized that he came alive in the pulpit! He was very reserved. He was a model citizen. His presence spoke for him. Dr. Reese's leadership motivated, inspired and challenged many locals to get involved in politics. It didn't just reach the city level, also extending to the state and the national level. I had the opportunity to serve as a state legislator and Terri Sewell is currently a U.S. congresswoman representing Selma. His legacy impacted a lot of us. Dr. Reese's leadership has bled over to impact our lives today. It would be impossible to do what we do if we didn't have courageous leaders such as Dr. Reese, who opened up true democracy for all Americans.*

*It is a humbling experience to know that I am serving in the capacity of Mayor. Knowing the rich history of Selma, we want to make sure this history aligns with the economic development we wish to take place in the city. While I am humbled by this position, we still face challenges in the 21st century in this great city, and it takes courageous leadership to address the economic challenges we face in this historic city.*

*Currently, the city of Selma is partnering with the Chamber of Commerce to lead the initiative of tourism in the* city of Selma. We are in the phase of discussing ways to boost and expand tourism through discussions with our Planning and Development Department. There will be extensive conversations between the Mayor's office and City Council members to try to create opportunities to expand tourism in the city. And we do see other opportunities. We want to be creative with our revenue in order to make certain optimal opportunities are created.

It is my hope that with the current administration and current council, we can find a way to make sure that Selma is one of the premier cities of the south as we move further into the 21st Century. At this time, we are focusing on technology infrastructure inside the city. Five years from now, I would like Selma to be known as the technology hub of the Black Belt region.

Selma is in the process of building our Interpretive Center, which has been a multiyear project. We've had conversations with the engineers and the Planning and Development Department about creating a space for Dr. Reese. We want to pay tribute to Dr. Reese and make him a part of the Historic Trail so that visitors can learn of his contribution to Selma's history.

Dr. Reese was a model leader. He was humble, always putting others before himself. He never sang his own praises. He was the leader of sacrifice. Many leaders throughout this country and throughout the world can learn from him. He didn't care about his name being mentioned. He wanted to make sure that others were lifted up by way of their own *unique circumstances. Instead of focusing on ourselves, we should focus on those we serve.*

*I believe Selma is the birthplace of true democracy. We didn't expand to a democracy until 1965, following the historic events that transpired in this small city. I don't see Selma as a city within the state of Alabama or a city within the United States. Rather, I see Selma as an international city, a city for all of the world.*

**Darrio Melton**
**Current Mayor of Selma, Alabama**

Below is a copy of the telegram received by Rev. Reese from Dr. Martin Luther King, Jr. on January 11, 1964.

JANUARY 11, 1964

*Selma*

TELEGRAM TO: Reverend F. D. Reece
●●●●●●●●●●
Selma, Alabama

I am strengthened in heart and in my work by your demonstration of yesterday. The protest of Dallas County teachers carried us miles down the road in the protest of injustices and at the same time up the road to the "Great Society". Most important, however, is the fact that you have destroyed the often made charge that teachers of a professional group is afraid to fight injustice. People all over the country are today standing on their feet applauding your action.

I thank you and congratulate you.

Martin Luther King, Jr

# FINAL WORDS

## OPEN LETTER
### Self-Sacrifice: The Message

Dear Friends,

As I recapitulate my life experiences, I surmise my path by paraphrasing the title of a book written by Maya Angelou, *Wouldn't Take Nothing for My Journey Now*. As for me, I haven't one regret. Orchestrating the Teachers March; inviting and extending the written invitation to Martin Luther King, Jr. and the SCLC to join Selma in the fight for justice; executing endless conversations to embrace peace; generating unfeigned prayers for those fighting for and against us; standing face-to-face with those oppressing and opposing us; discrediting the dismal prognosticators in their attempts to destroy us; marching across the Edmund Pettus Bridge on Bloody Sunday arm in arm singing, "We Shall Overcome;" witnessing my fellow brothers and sisters in the movement as they were brutally beaten with billy clubs, senselessly sprayed with tear gas, viciously kicked, and punched and spat on; spending long, dark nights in cold,

239

dismal jail cells while fighting for civil rights, not only for blacks, but for the civil rights of every man, woman and child, regardless of race, skin tone or skin color…the job had to be done.

Leading the Courageous Eight; maintaining my innocence when falsely accused of embezzlement, only to be completely vindicated; leading demonstrations against small Alabama businesses and protests against corporate giant Walmart during the late 1980s on the 4th of July for failing to hire qualified blacks in management positions; marrying the love of my life; losing two of our five children to muscular dystrophy; heeding the call of service as an ordained minister, pastoring Ebenezer Baptist Church for over 50 years; and meeting our esteemed 44th President of the United States of America, President Barack Obama, at the 50th Anniversary Commemorating Bloody Sunday, the Selma to Montgomery March, and the Voting Rights Acts of 1965. These are only snapshots of my lifelong accolades and accomplishments…the job had to be done.

Ecclesiastes 3:1-2 (NKJV) tells us, *To everything there is a season, a time for every purpose under heaven: a time to be born, and a time to die, a time to plant and a time to pluck what is planted.* I believe my accomplishments have been in direct alignment with my season, my time and my purpose. I thank God for my ability to hold steadfast to my faith. I know that I was appointed for a specific purpose, and I take solace in knowing that I am a child of the Most High God. I know that His grace, protection and mercy have allowed me to be a beacon of hope and a vessel of change for my beloved Selma.

God revealed to me that through it all, I've never been alone.

And because of that, I've never been afraid to stand. When you know you're right, you should stand. No matter how dark it gets, you must realize that after every night, there comes a day… Rest assured that all of our strength comes from God. And when you're left with nothing and you find yourself backed against a wall, just stand.

After you've fired your last shot and you realize that there are no more bullets in your gun, just stand. When you stand for what's right, it means you have love in your heart. Love is nondiscriminatory. Therefore, love has no color. I chose to stand for justice because the love I have in my heart encapsulates everyone, regardless of hue. And when you have that kind of love in your heart, your life will be blessed. And my God has blessed me beyond measure! For that, I am immensely and eternally grateful. I chose to stand because I was determined to be a soldier for what was right in God's sight. *"Stand therefore, having girded your waist with truth, having put on the breastplate of righteousness."* (Ephesians 6:14) NKJV. So, gird your loins, have your "feet shod with the preparation of the gospel of peace." (Ephesians 15:16) But, most of all, STAND! I will forever stand. My honor. My truth. My journey… Selma's Self-Sacrifice. May God continue to bless you all!

Sincerely,

Frederick D. Reese

# A NOTE FROM THE AUTHOR

I wish to thank the following, who contributed through interviews, support, insight and the provision of information: Althelstein Johnson, Stephen Posey (Selma-Dallas County Reference Staff), Carrie DeYampert-Grider, Mayor Darrio Melton (Mayor of Selma), Terri Sewell, (U.S. Representative for Alabama's 7th District), Caroline Robinson, George Duke Wilson, II, Nancy Sewell, Tina Smiley, Miranda Grass Manley and Rev. James Perkins, Jr.

The legacy of Rev. Dr. Frederick D. Reese is certain to live on in the lives of his family, friends and colleagues, and in everyone who loved and respected him. He touched and changed the lives

243

of so many. His self-sacrifice, dedication, determination and drive have left an indelible mark on the pavement, steps and sidewalks of Selma, and on the famous bridge over which he courageously marched.

I am both honored and humbled to have met him and to have witnessed his serene yet powerful aura, and I am sincerely grateful for the opportunity to have been in his presence. For I, too, have learned to "stand." It is with relentless certitude that I resonate the sentiments of many ... Rev. Dr. Frederick D. Reese was a great man!

A special thanks goes to the entire Reese Family: Alan, Kimberly, Marvin Sr., Frances, Marvin Jr., Charlene, Valerie R. Harris, Ed Harris, Christa, Demetrius and Lacrisca Dower and Tristan Nelson. I want to thank my beautiful parents, R.L. and Doris Walters, my siblings, my brothers-in-law, and my nieces and nephews and their parents, for supporting me beyond measure.

Finally, and most importantly, I thank God for this opportunity, for He orchestrated, anointed and ordained this entire project!

Writefully yours,

*Kathy M. Walters*

# REFERENCES

**Books**

Chestnut, J., & Cass, J. (1990). *Black in Selma*. New York: Farrar, Straus, and Giroux.

Vaughn, W., & Davis, M. (2006). *The Selma campaign, 1963-1965: The Decisive Battle of The Civil Rights Movement*. Dover, MA: Majority Press.

**Speech**

Lyndon B. Johnson's Speech- LBJ Presidential Library

http://www.lbjlibrary.org/press/lbj-in-the-news/the-american-promise-lbjs-finest-hour

**Interviews**

Crossley, C. (1985). *Interview of Reverend Frederick D. Reese conducted for Eyes on the Prize* [Recorded Sound]. Washington University in St. Louis Blackside, Inc. Retrieved from http://mavisweb.wulib.wustl.edu:81/mavisDetail/TitleWork/key/836

**Videos**

Diaz, F. (2010). *Meeting Dr. Frederick Douglas Reese in Selma,*

*Alabama* [Video]. Retrieved from https://www.youtube.com/ watch?v=fdVTMMqIEx0&t=26s

Fields, D. (2009). *Teachers in Selma March for the Right to Vote* [Video]. Retrieved from https://www.youtube.com/ watch?v=ikID6cE3ttI&t=45s

Fields, D. (2009). *Bloody Sunday* [Video]. Retrieved from https:// www.youtube.com/watch?v=miGSdabwu7Q&t=2s

Freedom Lifted (2013). *Rev. Frederick D. Reese: "Stand"* [Video]. Retrieved from https://www.youtube.com/watch?v=OwYW-vPLYTw

Freedom Lifted (2013). *Rev. Frederick Reese: "Stand"* [Video]. Retrieved from https://www.youtube.com/watch?v=OwYW-vPLYTw

Manley, M. (2018). *Dr. Frederick Reese was a teacher: An Oral History by Miranda Manley* [Video]. Retrieved from https:// www.youtube.com/watch?v=2RLiPP_95-I

The Grio (2013). *Rev. Frederick D. Reese remembers "Bloody Sunday" in Selma Part 2* [Video]. Retrieved from https://www. youtube.com/watch?v=QvoEVyKwtQc

The Grio (2013). *Reverend Frederick D. Reese Remembers Selma* [Video]. Retrieved from https://www.youtube.com/

watch?v=2Uz7UIUbFKE

**Additional References:**
Good Black News: https://goodblacknews.org/tag/rev-frederick-d-reese/

The Nation: https://www.thenation.com/article/fifty-years-after-march-selma-everything-and-nothing-has-changed/

Washington University in St. Louis-University Libraries: http://repository.wustl.edu/concern/videos/6m311r068

Eventbrite: https://www.eventbrite.com/e/march-4-muscles-tickets-54838265729

C-SPAN: https://www.c-span.org/video/?405070-1/congressional-gold-medal-ceremony-1965-voting-rights-marches-foot-soldiers

Selma Times Journal Searches

Google Searches

Personal Interviews

Wikipedia

# INDEX

52129464R00162

Made in the USA
Columbia, SC
01 March 2019